A Handcrafted
Christmas

Creating a Welcoming Home for the Holidays

Compiled by Dawn Anderson

Martingale™
& COMPANY

Credits

PRESIDENT
Nancy J. Martin

CEO
Daniel J. Martin

PUBLISHER
Jane Hamada

EDITORIAL DIRECTOR
Mary V. Green

EDITORIAL PROJECT MANAGER
Tina Cook

TECHNICAL EDITOR
Dawn Anderson

COPY EDITOR
Candie Frankel

DESIGN AND
PRODUCTION MANAGER
Stan Green

ILLUSTRATORS
Mary Newell DePalma, Roberta
Frauwirth, Michael Gellatly,
Nenad Jakesevic,
Jil Johänson, Judy Love

PHOTOGRAPHERS
Carl Tremblay,
Daniel van Ackere

COVER AND TEXT DESIGNER
Stan Green

Mission Statement

We are dedicated to providing
quality products and service by
working together to inspire
creativity and to enrich
the lives we touch.

Martingale™
& COMPANY

A Handcrafted Christmas: Creating a Welcoming Home
for the Holidays
© 2001 Martingale & Company

The credits that appear on the contents page are hereby made
a part of this copyright page.

Martingale & Company
20205 144th Avenue NE
Woodinville, WA 98072-8478 USA
www.martingale-pub.com

Printed in Singapore
06 05 04 03 02 01   8 7 6 5 4 3 2 1

Library of Congress Cataloging-in-Publication Data

Anderson, Dawn.
    A handcrafted christmas : creating a welcoming home for the
    holidays /compiled by Dawn Anderson.
        p. cm.
    ISBN 1-56477-408-2
        1. Christmas decorations. 2. Handicraft. I. Title.

TT900.C4 A517 2001
745.594'12—dc21   2001032995

CONTRIBUTORS

All color photography by Carl Tremblay, except as noted.

Beaded Stars and Sequined Icicles
Designers: Candie Frankel and Mary Ann Hall
Illustrator: Jil Johänson

Gilded Gingerbread Cookie Ornaments
Designer: Dawn Anderson
Illustrators: Nenad Jakesevic, Jil Johänson, and Roberta Frauwirth
Photographers: Carl Tremblay and Daniel van Ackere

Glittered Icicle Ornaments
Designer: Francoise Hardy
Illustrators: Jil Johänson and Roberta Frauwirth

Elegant Ribbon Tassel
Designer: Dawn Anderson
Illustrator: Mary Newell DePalma

Sugarplum Wreath
Designer: Francoise Hardy
Illustrator: Mary Newell DePalma

Checked Stockings
Designer: Dawn Anderson
Illustrators: Judy Love and Roberta Frauwirth

Iridescent Pocketed Stocking
Designer: Dawn Anderson
Illustrators: Judy Love and Roberta Frauwirth

Spiral Wire Topiary
Designer: Mary Ann Hall
Illustrator: Judy Love

Boxwood Welcome Tree
Designer: Dawn Anderson
Illustrators: Judy Love and Roberta Frauwirth

Diamond Cherub Ornaments
Designer: Dawn Anderson
Illustrator: Michael Gellatly

Gold Mesh Ornament
Designer: Dawn Anderson
Illustrator: Mary Newell DePalma

Rhinestone Partridge and Pear
Designer: Dawn Anderson
Illustrator: Mary Newell DePalma

Beaded Window Icicles
Designer: Elizabeth Cameron
Illustrators: Judy Love and Jil Johänson

Diamond Wreath with Kissing Ball
Designer: Dawn Anderson
Illustrator: Judy Love

Heirloom Angel Tree Topper
Designer: Francoise Hardy
Illustrators: Michael Gellatly and Roberta Frauwirth

Block-Print Gift Wrap
Designer: Laura McFadden
Illustrator: Jil Johänson

Lantern Gift Card
Designer: Carol Endler Sterbenz
Illustrator: Mary Newell DePalma

Contents

Introduction

A shimmering ornament, a welcoming wreath, a colorful stocking, a hand-wrapped gift—the traditional holiday symbols we display in our homes each year give Christmas its sparkle. When we celebrate the holidays with treasures made by our own hands, the spirit of the season acquires a heartfelt meaning that simply can't be bought.

From the front door to the fireplace to the top of the tree, you'll find wonderful ways to carry the magic of the holidays throughout your home in *A Handcrafted Christmas*. Seventeen step-by-step projects will help you add a touch of elegance and warmth to every room. And because many of these projects take only a few hours to complete, you can use them to shower family and friends with gifts so they can share in the season's magic, too.

Start with beautiful ornaments to embellish the tree, from classic beaded stars and sequined icicles to delightful—and edible!—gilded cookie ornaments, perfect for a few hours of fun in the kitchen with the kids. Welcome your holiday guests at the door with a distinctive boxwood tree or a diamond wreath, complete with kissing ball. Adorn the fireplace mantel with a trio of coordinating stockings, or spruce up an entryway or corner with a spiral topiary glistening with lights.

For gift giving, craft your own hand-stamped gift wrap with the charming reindeer design provided, or create a design all your own. Or make a clever Christmas card that is truly a gift in itself; this card unfolds into a small, box-style lantern that encases a votive candle.

A Handcrafted Christmas introduces you to several craft techniques—sewing, beading, wreath making, wire bending, and rubber stamping, to name a few. Choose projects that feature a familiar technique, or try your hand at something new.

Whether you're looking for home-decorating ideas or a special something for friends and loved ones, *A Handcrafted Christmas* will show you how easy it is to apply a handmade touch to the holidays and celebrate in style.

Beaded Stars and Sequined Icicles

One pattern will make a million different ornaments—
just change the beads.

by Candie Frankel and Mary Ann Hall

HERE'S A STAR DESIGN THAT WILL NEVER LOOK THE SAME TWICE. Just follow the basic directions with beads of your own choosing to come up with different colors and silhouettes. You can use pearls, iridescent beads, glass beads, or even exotic and vintage beads recycled from old costume jewelry. The star points can be crisp and sharp or rounded off like flower petals. When you're tired of making stars, try the swirling sequin and seed-bead icicles.

Materials

For each star:
♦ 80 to 100 beads in assorted sizes and colors
♦ 36-gauge beading wire

For each icicle:
♦ Large-hole seed or rocaille beads
♦ 5mm sequins
♦ 20-gauge craft wire

You'll also need:
6-spoke star template (page 9); 1" cone-shaped tip (e.g., unopened caulk nozzle, pastry tips); flat-nose pliers; round-nose pliers; wire cutter; tape measure; and soft fabric or grooved work surface.

Making the Beaded Star

1. **STRING CENTER CIRCLE.** Cut a 60" length of 36-gauge beading wire. String on six identical beads and slide to middle. Pass one end through all six beads again, and draw up into tight circle.

2. **STRING FIRST PETAL.** Line up an odd number of beads (for instance, five, seven, nine) symmetrically, making middle bead larger or more distinctive if you wish. Thread beads onto both wires, stopping one bead past middle bead. Thread remaining bead(s) onto one wire only (illustration A, facing page). Curve beaded strand back toward center circle and lay entire piece flat on template to check alignment (see page 9). If spokes do not match template, or petal appears warped or stressed, redesign sequence with more beads. If in doubt, always increase bead count. To secure first petal, pull single wire snug around circle wire (between two beads) and thread back through petal beads until both wires are reunited (illustration B, facing page).

3. **COMPLETE FIRST TIER.** Repeat step 2, but start stringing with bead before middle bead (illustration C, facing page). Check match against template. Repeat to form six interconnecting petals all around. Join last petal to first with single wire. End off with both wires emerging from first petal's middle bead.

4. **ADD STAR POINTS.** Line up an odd number of beads, once again making middle bead (star point) more distinctive. Thread beads onto both wires. Insert wires through second petal's middle bead, pull snug, and shape star point (illustration D, facing page). Repeat all around for six star points; work in a single-wire hanging loop at one point. End off.

Making the Sequined Icicle

1. **MAKE GRADUATED WIRE COIL.** Starting 1" from tip, wind 20-gauge craft wire tightly around cone-shaped tip 8 to 12 times. Slip this 1"-long coil off tip and clip from spool 1" beyond smallest coil. Gently pull each end to stretch coil to about 5".

2. **STRING BEADS AND SEQUINS.** At tapered end, bend and crimp wire back on itself by ⅛". String on four or five seed beads, and slide down to crimped tip (illustration E, left). Continue, but now add sequins between beads; string all sequin cups facedown, or add sequins in pairs with cups facing each other. When ½" of wire remains, make 90-degree bend and form hanging loop.

E. Coil wire and slide seed beads down to tip.

MAKING THE BEADED STAR

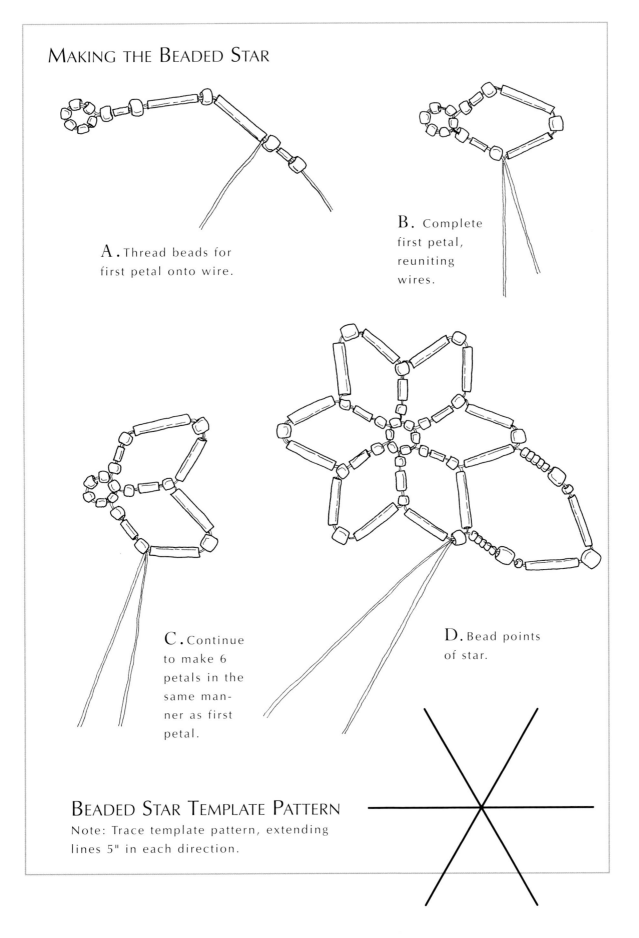

A. Thread beads for first petal onto wire.

B. Complete first petal, reuniting wires.

C. Continue to make 6 petals in the same manner as first petal.

D. Bead points of star.

BEADED STAR TEMPLATE PATTERN

Note: Trace template pattern, extending lines 5" in each direction.

Gilded Gingerbread Cookie Ornaments

These sparkling cookies can be used as ornaments,
but you can eat them, too.

by Dawn Anderson

LOOKING FOR A FAST AND EASY WAY TO DRESS UP YOUR HOLIDAY
gingerbread recipes? Consider this trio of metallic materials,
borrowed from the cake-decorating world: Luster Dust, an
edible metallic powder; edible glitter, made from gum arabic;
and gold dragées.

Luster Dust comes in gold, silver, or copper. You can
use the dust dry to add a light dusting of color or moisten it
with lemon extract and use it like watercolor paint. Edible
glitter, made from the same material as that used on the
back of envelopes, is available in a wide range of colors,
from gold and silver to red, green, and rainbow. The third
member of this metallic trio—dragées—is available in gold
and silver in a range of sizes.

To create the cookie shown in the photo, I started by
painting the gingerbread with liquefied gold Luster Dust,
then piped an outline and polka dots using white icing. Last,
I positioned gold dragées on the cookie and finished off with
a dusting of edible glitter.

Piped designs and gold dragées over liquefied gold Luster Dust

Painted with silver Luster Dust and embellished with piped icing and gold dragées

12

Materials

Yields twenty star cookies

Cookie Dough

- 3 cups all-purpose flour, sifted, plus extra for baking sheets and patterns
- 1 teaspoon baking soda
- 1½ teaspoons ground ginger
- 1½ teaspoons ground cinnamon
- ½ teaspoon ground nutmeg
- ½ teaspoon ground cloves
- ½ cup butter
- ½ cup dark brown sugar, firmly packed
- 1 egg
- ½ cup unsulfured molasses
- 1 tablespoon lemon juice

Icing/Decorations

- Egg white of one large egg
- 1 cup confectioners' sugar
- ½ teaspoon vanilla extract
- ¼ teaspoon cream of tartar
- Lemon extract
- Gold Luster Dust
- Gold dragées
- Edible glitter
- Narrow gold cord

You'll also need:
Star patterns (see page 15); two 2-ounce plastic squeeze bottles, each with coupler; cake decorating tips, sizes 1 and 2; electric mixer; sifter; large and small mixing bowls; medium-sized bowl; wet and dry measuring cups; measuring spoons; plastic wrap; waxed paper; tweezers; ruler; rolling pin; baking sheets; wire racks; paring knife; coffee mug; plate; ⅛"-diameter drinking straws; thin cardboard; glue-stick; scissors; custard cup or small glass jar; and small, new paintbrush.

Making the Gingerbread Ornaments

1. **MAKE STAR TEMPLATES.** Photocopy star patterns (see page 15 for patterns and enlargement instructions). Trim ½" beyond edges of the patterns (see page 15), then glue to cardboard. Cut along pattern outlines.

2. **MIX COOKIE DOUGH.** In medium-sized bowl, sift together flour, baking soda, ginger, cinnamon, nutmeg, and cloves; set aside. In large bowl, beat butter and brown sugar with mixer until fluffy. Mix in egg, molasses, and lemon juice. Add one-half dry ingredients and mix well, then add remaining dry ingredients and mix on low speed until combined. Divide dough in half. Form each half into ball, flatten slightly, and wrap with plastic wrap. Refrigerate 2 hours.

3. **CUT AND BAKE COOKIES.** Grease and lightly flour baking sheets. Place flattened dough balls on sheets, cover with wax paper, and roll to ⅛" thickness. Remove waxed paper. To cut cookies, dust cardboard template with flour, set on dough, and run paring knife along edge. If dough distorts, press knife blade straight down into dough instead of slicing through it, or rechill rolled dough 5 minutes to firm it up for cutting. Cut as many cookies as possible (illustration A). Gather up scrap dough and refrigerate for reuse. To make hanging hole, pierce tip of star point with straw approximately ¼" from edges. Refrigerate baking sheets with cut dough 15 minutes; preheat oven to 350 degrees. Bake cookies 8 to 10 minutes, taking care not to overbake. Transfer cookies to wire racks and let cool.

4. **PREPARE ICING.** In a small mixing bowl, beat egg white, confectioners' sugar, vanilla, and cream of tartar until smooth and peaks begin to form. Transfer icing to two 2-ounce squeeze bottles and cap with size 1 and 2 tips. Set bottles upside down in mug.

5. **APPLY LUSTER DUST.** Place ½ teaspoon lemon extract in custard cup or jar, add small amount of gold Luster Dust, and stir with brush to consistency of watercolor paint. Brush mixture across surface of each cookie for opaque coverage. If mixture is too watery, add more Luster Dust; if mixture becomes dry, add more lemon extract (illustration B).

13

A. Cut the star-shaped cookies using a cardboard template.

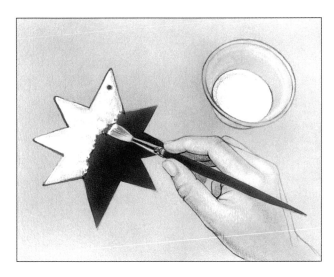

B. After baking, "gild" each cookie with liquefied Luster Dust.

14

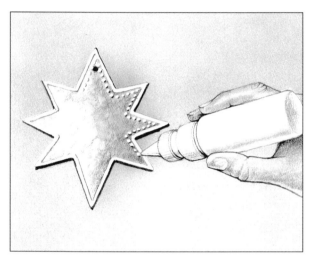

C. Pipe the icing, using a squeeze bottle for maximum control.

D. Sprinkle the cookie surface with edible glitter.

6. **ADD ICING AND DRAGÉES.** To start icing flow, shake bottle down sharply once or twice; store upside down in mug when not in use. Referring to design on template (see patterns on facing page) and using size 2 tip for lines and size 1 tip for dots, pipe icing onto cookie surface. Hold squeeze bottle at 45-degree angle with tip 1/8" above surface (illustration C). To add dragées, pipe dot of icing onto cookie, then set dragée into position with tweezers while icing is still wet. Let icing harden 20 minutes.

7. **APPLY EDIBLE GLITTER AND HANGING CORD.** Place cookie on waxed paper. Crush glitter between fingers, sprinkling it over entire cookie (illustration D). Shake cookie gently from side to side to distribute glitter, then turn cookie upside down to shed excess. Save for reuse. Repeat process for each cookie. To hang cookies, thread 8" length of gold cord through hole and tie off. Slide knot behind hole.

Designer's Tips

• To prevent the distortion that comes when shapes are transferred, roll out the dough directly on the baking sheet. If your baking sheet has rims that will interfere with rolling, turn it over and use the other side.

• After you've gathered up the scraps from the first batch of gingerbread dough, refrigerate them while you work with the remaining half. Continue alternating with each half until you've cut all the cookie designs.

• For straight, even lines when piping the icing, move the squeeze bottle quickly and smoothly. Do not let the tip of the bottle touch the surface of the cookie.

GILDED GINGERBREAD
COOKIE ORNAMENT
PATTERNS

Note: Photocopy pattern at 200% to make star 7¼" from top arrow to bottom arrow.

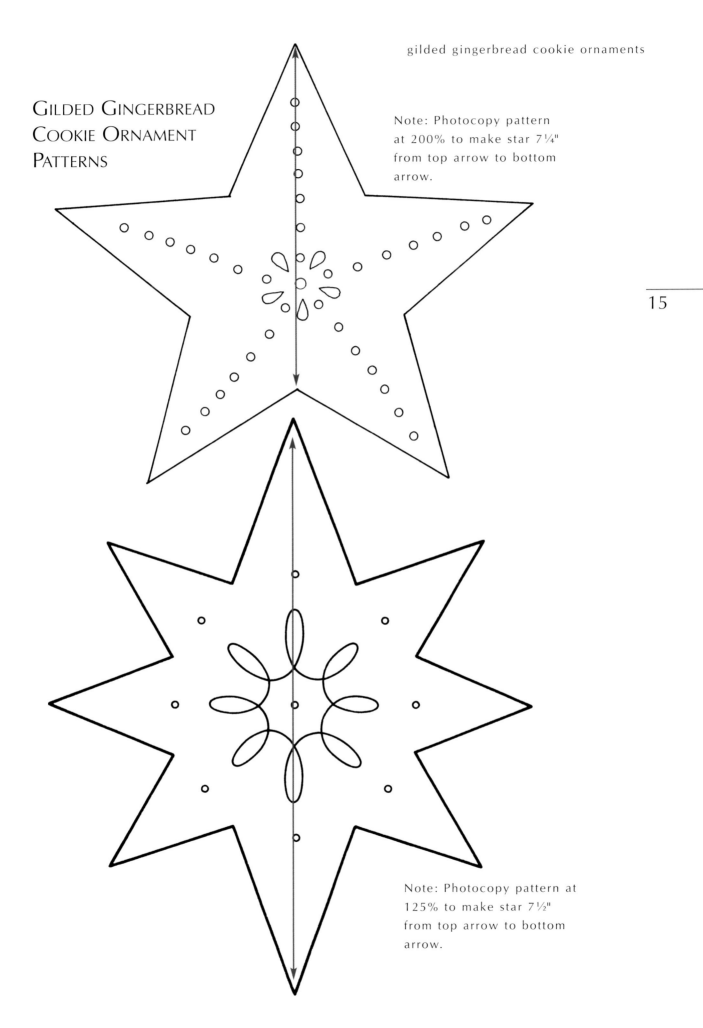

Note: Photocopy pattern at 125% to make star 7½" from top arrow to bottom arrow.

Glittered Icicle Ornaments

Twist dazzling ornaments from child-friendly thermoplastic strips softened in warm water.

by Francoise Hardy

THESE ICICLE ORNAMENTS ARE MADE FROM FRIENDLY PLASTIC, a thermoplastic with a low melting point that comes in both pellet and strip form. The strips are available in many colors and patterns, the best of which, in my opinion, are the mirrored-looking metallics. They come in glowing colors like fuchsia, hot pink, peridot, gold, and sky blue and resemble the shiny surfaces of hand-blown glass ornaments.

To begin, cut your plastic into tapered strips and heat a pot of water. Use a candy thermometer to maintain a water temperature of about 150 degrees, which is perfect for softening the plastic. If the water gets too hot, the plastic will become viscous, sticky, and impossible to shape. You can easily adjust the temperature by adding cold water or ice.

Working in sections makes it easier to shape the helix; practice the twisting on a few sample pieces until you get the hang of it. I curved my strip into a J-shape and heated and twisted one third at a time, starting at the wide end and working down. This way, you can also avoid heating the ends that you hold, leaving them free from fingerprints or bends. The twisted sections will harden on their own, or you can hasten the process by dipping each finished section in cold water. If your twists end up uneven, you may be able to reheat and reshape your icicle a few more times.

To complete the ornament, use a small brush to coat the nonreflective back and edges with Mod Podge, then dust the surfaces with micro glitter. After the icicle is dry, seal it with a clear gloss acrylic spray finish to bind any loose glitter and heighten the mirror shine of the plastic finish, which tends to lose some luster during the hot-water dipping process. Avoid using lacquer, which will strip the glitter and the mirror finish.

Materials

Makes twenty icicle ornaments

CUTTING
DIAGRAM

- Five 1½" x 7" Friendly Plastic strips in metallic colors
- Micro glitter in assorted colors
- Mod Podge
- Acrylic spray sealer (gloss)
- Thin gold elastic cord

You'll also need:
Cutting diagram (left); low 4-quart stockpot; candy thermometer; X-Acto knife; self-healing cutting mat; awl; steel ruler; sharp scissors; paper clips or wire ornament hangers; string drying line; ⅜" flat brush; and scrap paper.

Making the Icicle Ornaments

1. **CUT PLASTIC.** Lay one plastic strip dull side up on flat work surface. Refer to cutting diagram (left). Using X-Acto knife, steel ruler, and cutting mat, score strip in half lengthwise, then score diagonal line through each half, offsetting slightly so tapered end is blunt rather than sharply pointed. Cut on score lines with scissors. Cut straight across broad end to even up angles. Repeat process to cut 20 icicles total.

2. **SHAPE ICICLES.** Fill stockpot with water. Heat water to 150 degrees, monitoring temperature with candy thermometer. If water exceeds 150 degrees, remove from heat source and/or cool with ice cubes. Hold one strip by ends, with broader end in your left hand and mirrored side face up, and flex into J shape. Lower bottom of J into water (do not submerge broad end) and hold for 10 to 15 seconds to soften plastic to al dente pasta stage. Lift strip, straighten it, then rotate ends in opposite directions for 1 to 1½ twists; do not overtwist (illustration A, facing page). Hold under dribbling cold tap water a few seconds to set. Repeat process once or twice to soften, and twist remainder of strip into a continuous helix. Repeat to twist each plastic strip.

3. **APPLY GLITTER.** Using awl, pierce hole in broad end of each icicle. Suspend icicles temporarily with opened paper clips or ornament hangers. For each icicle, brush thin coat of Mod Podge on dull side and edges, and sprinkle with coordinating glitter, catching and reserving excess on scrap paper (illustration B, facing page). Hang icicles on string line and let dry overnight. Seal with acrylic spray, following manufacturer's instructions. To make permanent hangers, thread gold elastic cord through the hole and knot to make a loop.

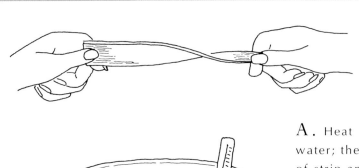

A. Heat plastic in hot water; then hold ends of strip and twist.

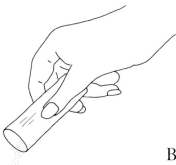

B. Sprinkle icicles with micro glitter.

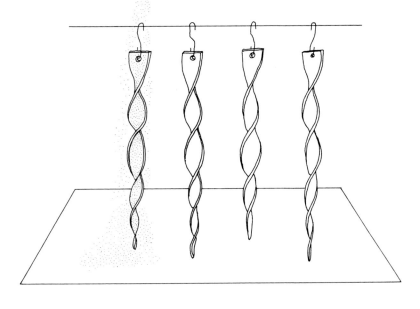

Elegant Ribbon Tassel

Substitute wood findings for a knotted top, and knitting tape for fringe.

by Dawn Anderson

TO MAKE THE HEAD OF THE TASSEL, I GLUED TOGETHER TWO candlecups with a small wooden disk in between, then painted it. To make the ribbon "tassel strings," I created a fringe and then rolled the fringe into a tassel shape. Last, I glued the rolled fringe into the large candlecup on the painted tassel head.

Materials

Makes one ornament

- 9⅝ yards ¼"-wide variegated picot-edged ribbon
- 1 yard silk embroidery ribbon to match variegated ribbon
- Thread to match ribbon
- 1¼" wood candlecup
- ⅝" wood candlecup
- ¾"-diameter wooden disk
- 2-ounce acrylic paints in the following colors: buttermilk, crimson, light green, and black
- 1-ounce container gold acrylic enamel paint
- Clear acrylic spray sealer with gloss finish
- Wood glue

You'll also need:
¾" flat brush; ⅛" and ¼" flat shader brushes; small round brush; small, stiff brush; fine-line paint syringe; watercolor palette or disposable plastic lid; 220-grit sandpaper; 600-grit wet and dry sandpaper; paper towels; painter's tape; sewing machine; iron and ironing board; hand-sewing needle; thin-gauge wire; 18-gauge floral stem wire; scissors; pencil; spray mister; ruler; and florist foam brick.

Making the Tassel Head

1. **GLUE WOOD PIECES.** With small, stiff brush, apply wood glue to open end of smaller candlecup and one side of disk. Press together and let set. Repeat to glue larger candlecup to disk (illustration A). Let dry 1 hour. Sand with 220-grit sandpaper. Wipe dust with lightly misted paper towel.
2. **PAINT BASE COAT.** Using ¾" flat brush, apply three coats buttermilk acrylic paint to wood surfaces; let dry 20 minutes between coats, propping tassel head on a piece of floral stem wire inserted into florist foam brick. Sand lightly with 600-grit sandpaper after third and fourth coats.
3. **PAINT STRIPES AND DETAILS.** Use the color photograph on page 20 as a reference for the painting steps. Use ¼" and ⅛" flat shader and small, round brushes for larger areas and stripes; use syringe for dots. Let dry 1 hour. Apply sealer, following manufacturer's instructions.

Attaching the Ribbon Tassel

1. **SEW RIBBON FRINGE.** Lower sewing-machine needle to down position, measure 2⅞" to right of needle, and lay strip of painter's tape on machine bed as guide. Measure and cut fifty 6½" lengths of picot-edged ribbon. Set remaining piece (about 20" long) on machine bed to serve as base ribbon, and lower needle into one end. Fold one cut ribbon length in half on machine bed, with fold on tape guide and loose ends crossing base ribbon in front of needle. Machine-stitch through all layers. Fold new cut ribbon, place adjacent to first ribbon, and continue stitching. Repeat process to sew all cut ribbons to base ribbon (illustration B).

A. Glue the wood pieces together.

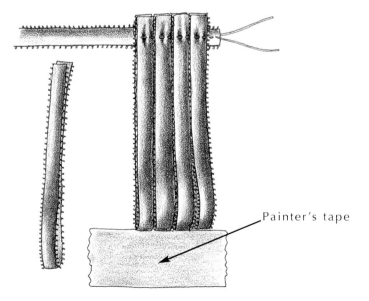

Painter's tape

B. Sew sections of ribbon to make fringe.

2. **ROLL FRINGE.** Using warm iron, press ribbon fringe, stopping ¼" from folds. Measure 3" section of base ribbon. Roll 3" section snugly, with base ribbon on outside, and hand-tack. Continue rolling and tacking 3" segments. As you near end, trim excess ribbon 1" beyond fringe, wrap securely, and hand-tack.

3. **MAKE TASSEL CORD.** Cut two 18" lengths of silk embroidery ribbon, then cut twelve 18" lengths of matching sewing thread. Hold all lengths of ribbon and thread together and knot one end. Hold knotted end steady and begin twisting other end. As soon as cord begins to kink and twist on itself, fold cord in half, hold ends together, and allow cords to spiral together. Tie knot 6" from folded end; trim excess close to knot.

4. **ASSEMBLE TASSEL.** Cut 8" length of thin wire, fold in half, and loop through unknotted end of tassel cord. Using wire, draw cord through small opening at top of tassel head until knot lodges inside, then remove wire. Apply wood glue inside tassel head and around top of ribbon tassel. Insert tassel into head (illustration C). If necessary, push stray ribbon ends up into tassel head using needle. Let glue dry overnight.

23

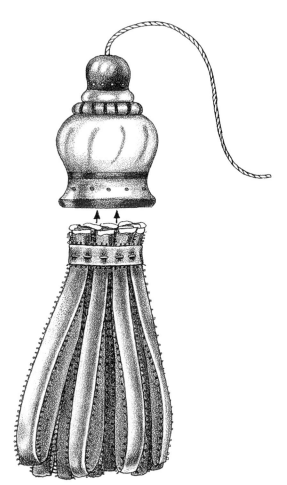

C. Roll the fringe and glue it into the head.

Sugarplum Wreath

The secret: Use road-sign reflective beads to add sparkle to the fruits.

by Francoise Hardy

To GIVE THE FRUITS ON THIS WINTRY GRAPEVINE WREATH THEIR lustrous appearance, I used two materials: a coat of iridescent metallic craft paint and tiny, clear reflective beads. These inexpensive glass beads, sold for making reflective signs, are classier than the plastic "snow" usually used in holiday crafts.

The best fruit to use for this project is made of styrene. It's lightweight, durable, takes paint well, and is easily embedded with wire. Hard plastic fruit will also work, but soft, rubbery neoprene fruits don't hold the glass beads well.

The fruit surface must be smooth for the metallic paint layer to shine. Plastic peaches can be defuzzed easily by soaking, but unfortunately this method will not dissolve the glues used on styrene peaches. You can always smooth a fuzzy skin with several coats of gesso, but it's easier to avoid flocked peaches and use smooth-skinned nectarines instead. Some newer hard-shell fruits, especially those with a very matte, della Robbia–style finish, are coated with a thin latex film that resists painting. It will be obvious immediately if your fruit has this coating when you prick it with a needle or an X-Acto blade tip. If the latex layer separates, lift and peel it off as a whole sheet. The painted surface underneath can then be painted with no further preparation.

For a visually interesting wreath, include fruits like pears and pomegranates that have distinctive silhouettes or details. Also use different sizes, including large and small versions of the same fruit. Although I didn't use them, limes and lemons are also suitable choices. Grapes or berries can be used in small clusters to add filler where needed. Finally, use velvet leaves to add a soft background.

To achieve a light and airy look, I used only twelve main fruits and arranged them around a grapevine base that was delicate rather than dense in appearance. To style my own wreath, I separated a few vines from a purchased wreath and wound them loosely around a wire wreath form. As you assemble your wreath, give each fruit "breathing room," and spin the tendrils toward the surrounding space. Finish the wreath with subtle highlights of bronze paint and glitter to camouflage any joins or blemishes and to give the wreath a dewy glow.

Materials

Makes one 20" sugarplum wreath

♦ 12 assorted 2" to 4" artificial fruits
♦ 1 bunch artificial grapes
♦ 2 stems with 1" fruits
♦ 4 to 5 stems with small berries
♦ 20 assorted 2" to 4" flocked velvet leaves
♦ 14" to 18" grapevine wreath
♦ 16" flat wire wreath form
♦ 1 pint Rolco Labs reflective beads (see "Sources" on page 96)
♦ 24-gauge fabric-covered wire
♦ 1 package of 20-gauge, 18" brown paper-covered stems
♦ Brown florist tape
♦ Bronze micro glitter
♦ Assorted metallic paints, 2 ounces each: Plaid Folk Art Bronze 663, Copper 664, Peach Pearl 674, Peridot 671, Periwinkle 669, Plum 668, Rose Shimmer 652, Accent Crown Jewels Imperial Antique Gold 2528
♦ Mod Podge (gloss)

You'll also need:
Hot-glue gun; 16-gauge steel wire; wire cutters; ⅝", ½" , and ⅜" dowels; 1" foam brush; ½" flat soft-bristle brush; small sponge; candle and matches; wide-mouthed 1-quart container; large bowl; and twist-ties.

Making the Fruits

1. **MAKE WIRE HOLDERS.** Cut twelve 12" lengths of 16-gauge wire. For each medium and large fruit, choose side with interesting details or contours to face outward on wreath, e.g., split of peach, belly of pear, stem of apple. Join wire to opposite side as follows: Curve end of wire slightly, heat curved section in candle flame, and push into fruit so it emerges 1" to 2" away. The hot wire will glide easily through the foam fruit. Let cool 5 minutes, then twist wire ends together. Use wire as handle when painting and paving fruits, and as hanger when drying.

2. **PAINT FRUITS.** Using ½" flat brush, apply metallic paint to each fruit (except grapes) according to its natural color. Let dry, then brush or sponge in shading and highlights. For example, paint a nectarine gold or peach and blush it with copper or rose; paint a pear green, then add gold highlights on one side to suggest sun ripening. Don't worry if shading does not blend realistically, since glass reflective beads will soften harsh lines. Paint small berries periwinkle. Hang fruits and let dry 1 hour.

3. **Pave fruits with glass beads.** Transfer reflective beads to wide-mouthed container, to create a fan-shaped spill when poured. Using foam brush, spread Mod Podge evenly on one large fruit. With bowl underneath to catch excess, pour beads in gentle stream over wet fruit, turning it for complete coverage. Hold back glass dust at end of pour and discard it. Check that all areas are coated, then hang to dry. Repeat process for all fruits except berries; cut grapes into three or four small clusters and pave each cluster. Be careful not to nudge or disturb coated fruit, and do not let hanging fruits touch one another. Let dry overnight.

Making the Wreath Base

1. **Wind grapevines on wire wreath form.** Untwine grapevine wreath. If vines are extremely brittle and prone to breaking, soak entire wreath in basin of water for 1 hour or more, until more pliable. Wind a few vines around wreath form, just enough to give it some coverage while retaining light, airy look (illustration A). Hold temporarily with twist-ties; if vines are wet, let wreath air-dry overnight.

    Permanently secure vines to wreath form in four or five spots using wire and/or hot glue.

A. Wind a grapevine around a wire wreath form.

2. **PAINT GRAPEVINE WREATH.** Using $\frac{1}{2}$" flat brush, apply bronze paint randomly to vines and wreath form. For lustrous effect, do not attempt to paint every surface. Let dry 20 minutes.

3. **MAKE TENDRILS.** Coil 18" brown paper-covered stem around a dowel for 3" to 4"; then coil back in other direction around dowel of different diameter. Push and pull finished coil to create natural-looking tendril. Repeat process to make five or six tendrils total. Set tendrils aside.

Assembling the Wreath

1. **WIRE FRUITS TO WREATH.** Remove wire holder from each fruit and replace with 12" length of fabric-covered wire. Adjust so both ends extend evenly, then twist wires together close to fruit surface. Tentatively place twelve fruits around wreath, arranging them so like colors, sizes, and shapes are not adjacent. Once arrangement is set, wire fruits to inner or outer wreath to create undulating path. To secure each fruit, twist wires together at back of wreath, clip off excess, and bind with florist tape (illustration B). Fill in bare spaces with 1" fruits, grape clusters, and berries; to attach them, wind stems around grapevine for a few inches and bind with florist tape. Keep overall look open and airy, rather than lush or cluttered (illustration C).

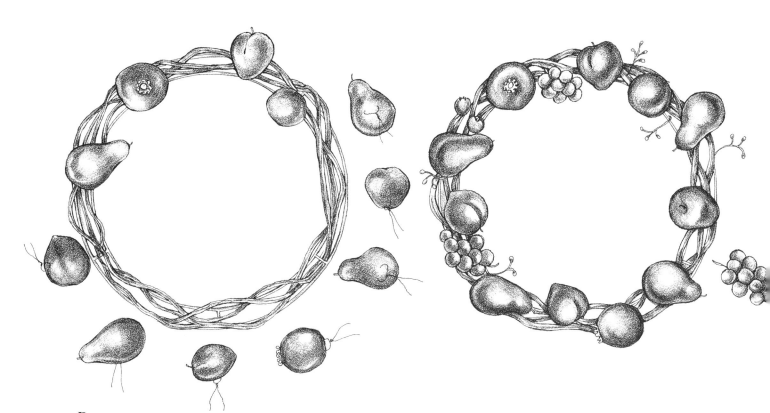

B. Arrange the fruits and wire them to the wreath.

C. Add the smaller fruits, grape clusters, and berries.

2. **ADD TENDRILS AND LEAVES.** Attach tendrils and leaves in same manner as berries, by winding stem around grapevine and binding with florist tape. To extend or strengthen existing leaf stems, lay stem wire along existing stem and bind both stems together tightly with florist tape. Use leaves as camouflage to hide any exposed fruit wires, unattractive joins, or the wire wreath form. Position leaves so larger, darker leaves recede toward back and smaller, lighter leaves loft forward. Use longer stems to advantage to float leaves where you need them. To garnish a fruit, remove the plastic stem, insert the leaf stem in the opening, and rejoin the plastic stem with hot-glue. Wrap any areas of wreath form that remain visible with florist tape. Use short strips for easier handling, and wrap loosely to suggest woody vines (illustration D).

3. **ADD SPARKLE.** Using flat brush and bronze paint, touch up any stem joins or other taped areas that could use camouflaging. Apply thin coat of Mod Podge at random to vines, tendrils, and leaf stems that are visible and easily reached. Sprinkle bronze micro glitter over these areas, rubbing pinches of it between your fingertips to release very light snowfall. To make a hanging loop, shape a wire stem wrapped with brown florist tape and attach it to wreath back.

29

D. Use leaves and tendrils to fill out the bare spots.

Checked Stockings

Jazz up your mantel with stockings sewn from
unconventional patterns and fabrics.

by Dawn Anderson

THIS YEAR, MAKE STOCKINGS WITH UNEXPECTED STYLE AND FLAIR.
Start by selecting a fabric with a striking multicolor check, such as
the vibrant silk dupioni featured here. Checks, while often traditional or country in style, can be quite contemporary when woven
in bold, zesty colors. In silk, they can also be elegant.

To coordinate a set of checked stockings, make each cuff from a different
solid-colored fabric that matches one of the check colors.

For a final touch, make unique cuff accents out of brass chains and glass beads.
You can make swag-style accents by tacking the beaded decoration to both side
seams, or you can make fringe-style embellishments that hang from just one side
of the cuff.

Materials

Makes three 12"-long stockings

- 45"-wide silk dupioni:
  1 yard multicolor check (body)
  ⅞ yard oasis (lining + one cuff)
  ⅓ yard crimson (cuff)
  ⅓ yard turquoise (cuff)
- 2⅔ yard 60"-wide fusible tricot interfacing
- Thread to match fabrics
- Assorted glass beads:
  Three 16mm to 34mm
  Two 12mm to 16mm
  Five 9mm
  Fourteen 3mm
- 28" brass jewelry chain
- Three ⅜" brass rings
- Head pins
- Eye pins

You'll also need:
Stocking pattern (see page 35); sewing machine; iron; round-nose jewelry pliers; chain-nose jewelry pliers; wire cutter; sewing shears; hand-sewing needle; pins; and pencil.

Making the Stockings

1. **CUT FABRICS.** From checked silk, cut six stockings, reversing three (see Designer's Tip on page 34). From oasis (lime green) silk, cut six stockings for lining (reverse three). Cut one 9½" x 14¾" cuff each from oasis, crimson, and turquoise silk, short edge parallel to selvage. From tricot interfacing, cut six stockings (reverse three) and three cuffs. Fuse interfacing to wrong side of checked stockings and solid cuffs, following manufacturer's instructions.

2. **SEW STOCKINGS AND LININGS.** Pin each checked stocking pair right sides together. Stitch curved edge, making ½" seam. Trim seam allowance to a scant ¼". Stitch each oasis lining pair in same way, increasing seam allowance to ¾" around foot and leaving a 4" opening on back seam for turning as per pattern (illustration A). Turn checked stockings right side out and press well. Trim but do not turn linings.

3. **SEW CUFFS.** Fold each cuff in half lengthwise, wrong side in, and press to set fold. Unfold, pin short edges right sides together, and stitch ½" from edge. Trim seam allowance and press seam open. Refold along previous fold and baste raw edges together (illustration B). Pin cuff to upper edge of each checked stocking, matching raw edges and back seam. Baste ⅜" from edge all around.

A. Sew each stocking and lining pair.   **B.** Assemble each cuff.

4. **ASSEMBLE STOCKINGS.** Slip checked stocking inside lining stocking, right sides together (illustration C). Match top edges and pin. Machine-stitch ½" from edge all around through all layers (illustration D). Trim seam allowance. Turn lining right side out by pulling checked stocking through opening. Slipstitch opening closed (illustration E). Push lining down inside stocking, and press upper cuff edge. Hand-tack one brass ring to back of cuff for hanging.

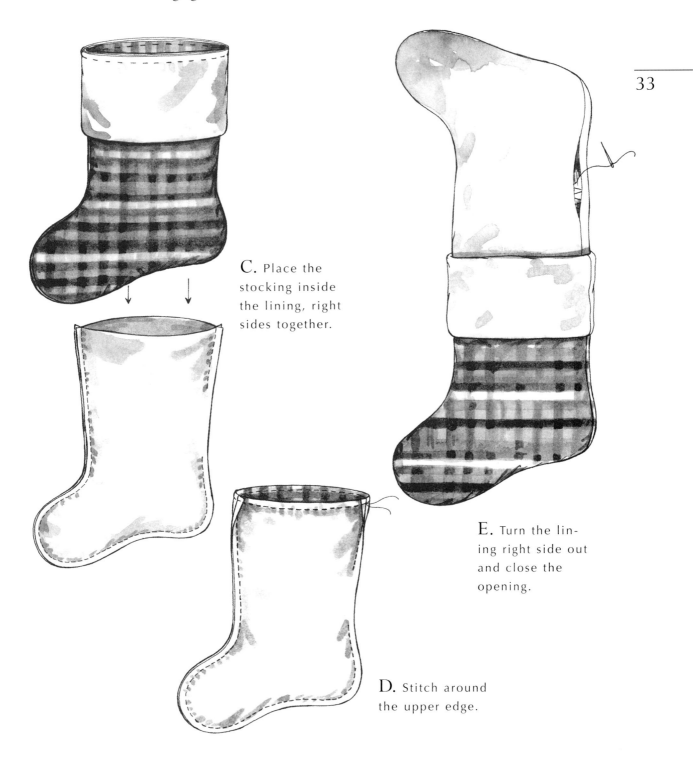

C. Place the stocking inside the lining, right sides together.

D. Stitch around the upper edge.

E. Turn the lining right side out and close the opening.

5. **ADD BEADED CHAINS.** Try the embellishment ideas below or create your own designs. To make a beaded drop (see how-to illustration, below), thread the bead(s) onto a head or eye pin; bend the pin wire down 90 degrees and clip to leave a ⅜" tail. Use round-nose pliers to shape this tail into a loop. Pry the loop open with chain-nose pliers to attach the drop to a chain link or another drop.

    Oasis cuff: Make two drops, each with a 3mm bead and a 12mm to 16mm accent bead. Attach a drop to each end of a 12" chain. Hand-tack chain to inside top cuff so beads dangle down sides of stocking.

    Turquoise cuff: Hand-tack 8" chain to inside cuff so chain drapes across cuff front. Make five drops by threading 9mm bead on eye pin. Attach drops across chain. Thread a 3mm bead on each of nine head pins. Attach five to existing drops, and attach remaining four to chain in between (illustration F).

Designer's Tip

Cut one checked stocking, then flip it over and use it as a template to cut the mate. You'll be able to match the checks and colors perfectly.

F. Decorate the cuff with chains and beaded drops.

    Crimson cuff: Make three drops, each with a 3mm bead and a 16mm to 34mm accent bead on a head pin. Attach drops to 3", 2⅝", and 2⅜" chains. Tack all three chains to inside cuff on front side.

Making a Beaded Drop

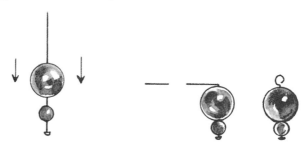

CHECKED STOCKING PATTERN

NOTE: Photocopy pattern at 200%.

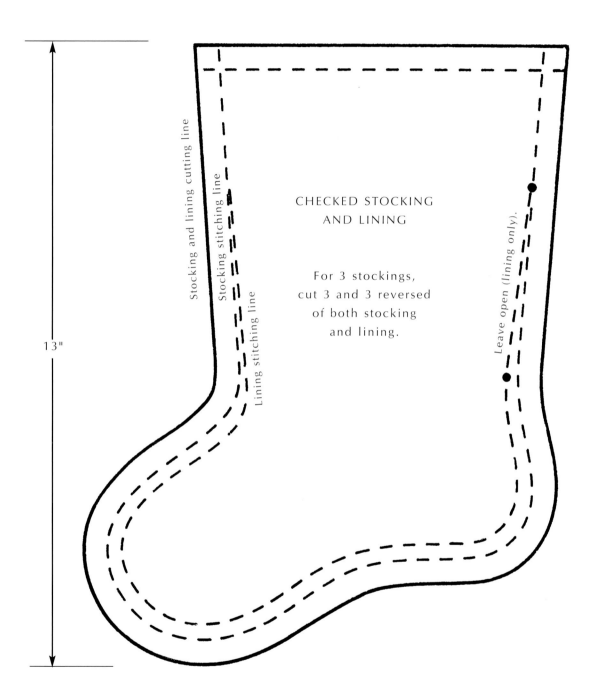

13"

Stocking and lining cutting line

Stocking stitching line

Lining stitching line

CHECKED STOCKING
AND LINING

For 3 stockings,
cut 3 and 3 reversed
of both stocking
and lining.

Leave open (lining only).

Iridescent Pocketed Stocking

Use luscious fabrics and high-voltage colors to create dramatic Christmas stockings.

by Dawn Anderson

TIRED OF PREDICTABLE HOLIDAY COLORS? MAKE THIS THE YEAR you venture beyond reds and greens to a brilliant pastel palette. I chose hot pink for my pocketed stocking design, but you could also use fuchsia, apricot, gold, chartreuse, or even teal. When sewn from shimmering iridescent fabrics—silk dupioni and sheer organza—these stockings will transform your hearth with their dramatic presence.

Most of the stocking assembly is done on the sewing machine, but for a fast finish, the sheer pocket is attached with fusible tape. Be sure to use a press cloth or heavy cotton fabric when ironing the tape to the organza. Without it, the heated glue may ooze through the organza, leaving a residue on your sole-plate or ironing board cover.

Materials

Makes one 19"-long stocking

- ¾ yard 45"-wide iridescent pink-red silk dupioni
- ½ yard 45"-wide fuchsia-gold metallic organza
- ¼ yard ⅝"-wide pink grosgrain ribbon
- ⅝ yard 20"-wide fusible knit interfacing
- Thread to match fabrics
- ½"-wide iron-on adhesive tape

You'll also need:
Stocking pattern (see page 41); sewing machine; iron and ironing board; sewing shears; press cloth; grid ruler; hand-sewing needle; and pins.

Making the Pocketed Stocking

1. **CUT CUFF AND POCKET PIECES.** From organza, cut one 10½" x 14½" rectangle for cuff and one 4¼" x 5½" rectangle for pocket.

2. **CUT STOCKING PIECES.** From pink-red silk dupioni, cut four stockings (reverse two). From interfacing, cut two stockings (reverse one). Fuse interfacing to wrong side of two stockings, following manufacturer's directions.

3. **SEW STOCKING AND LINING.** Pin interfaced stockings right sides together. Stitch curved edge, making ½" seam. Trim seam allowance to a scant ¼"; notch convex curves and clip concave curves. Pin two remaining stockings right sides together for lining. Stitch curved edge, increasing seam allowance to ¾" around foot and leaving 4" opening on back seam as shown on pattern. Trim seam allowances (illustration A).

4. **SEW CUFF.** Fold organza cuff in half lengthwise, wrong side in; press to set fold. Unfold, pin short edges right sides together, and stitch ½" from edge. Trim seam allowance to ¼"; press seam open. Refold along previous fold, and baste raw edges together (illustration B).

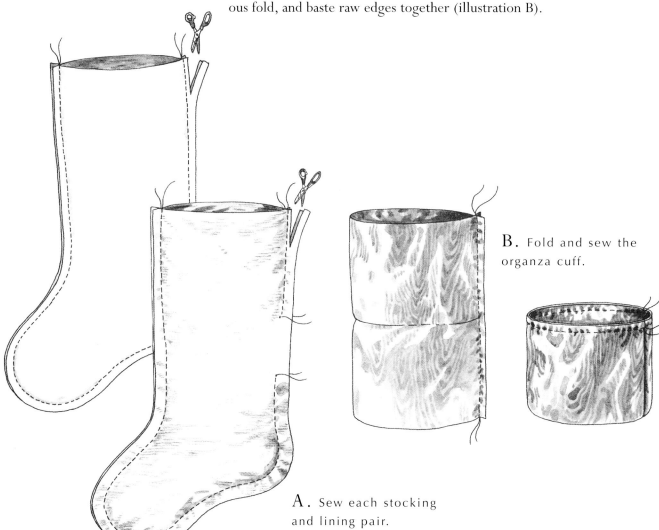

B. Fold and sew the organza cuff.

A. Sew each stocking and lining pair.

5. **ASSEMBLE STOCKING.** Press stocking seam open, turn right side out, and press well. Pin cuff to upper edge, matching back seam. Fold 6" length of ribbon in half, and pin ends, raw edges matching, over cuff seam. Hand-baste ⅜" from edge all around. Slip stocking inside lining, right sides together (illustration C). Pin top edges together. Machine-stitch ½" from edge all around, trapping cuff and ribbon hanger in seam (illustration D). Pull stocking through opening and turn lining right side out.

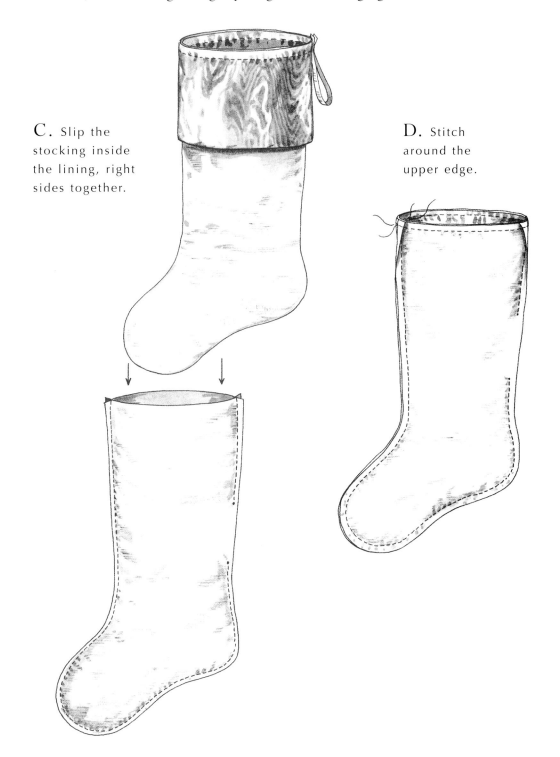

C. Slip the stocking inside the lining, right sides together.

D. Stitch around the upper edge.

E. Turn right side out. Fuse the pocket to the stocking front.

6. **ADD POCKET.** Following manufacturer's instructions, fuse 4½" length of adhesive tape to corresponding pocket edge. Fold down edge ½" (even with tape) and press. Repeat to make double-fold hem for pocket top. Press three remaining raw edges ¼" to wrong side. Cut ¼"-wide strips of adhesive tape and fuse to folded edges. Fuse pocket to stocking front, as indicated on pattern. Slipstitch lining opening closed (illustration E). Push lining down inside stocking. Fold down cuff and press upper edge.

Designer's Tip

Iridescent fabric is woven from two different thread colors. Either one can show and shimmer to advantage, depending on the fabric's drape and orientation. Decide which orientation you prefer and lay out the pattern pieces accordingly.

IRIDESCENT POCKETED STOCKING PATTERN

NOTE: Photocopy pattern at 250%

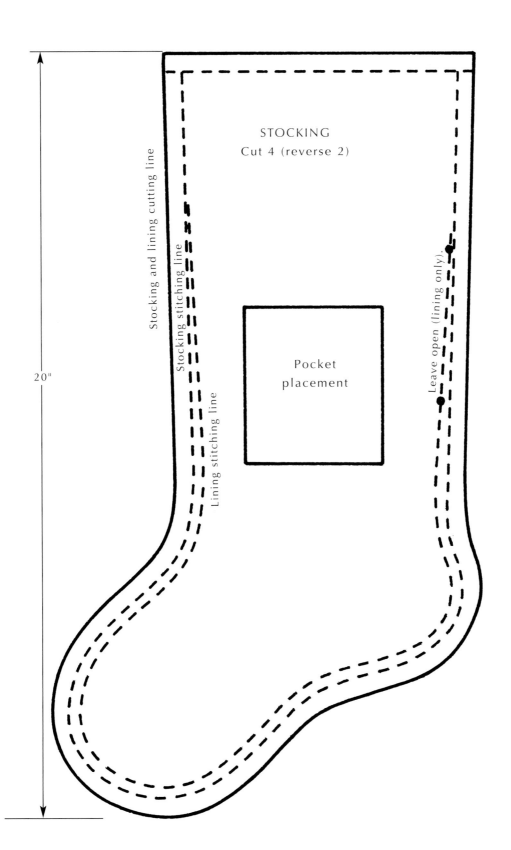

STOCKING
Cut 4 (reverse 2)

Pocket
placement

Stocking and lining cutting line

Stocking stitching line

Lining stitching line

Leave open (lining only)

20"

Spiral Wire Topiary

Recycle common household supplies into a glamorous holiday sculpture.

by Mary Ann Hall

I LOVE THE SLEEK APPEAL OF MODERN WIRE CHRISTMAS TREES, but the ones I've seen in catalogs and magazines have cost close to $100. With a little ingenuity, you can create the same look for about $6. Just shape a simple framework from vinyl-coated wire and decorate it with the dazzling ornaments of your choice.

The trunk of my tree is a 49¢ garden stake. To support the stake, I mixed up some plaster of Paris in a 1-quart yogurt container and embedded the stake directly in it. I hid the base inside a silver ice bucket. You might want to decide on your outside container first, then select a disposable container that will fit inside. (See Designer's Tips on page 46 for more ideas.)

Use 14-gauge steel wire to hand-shape the conelike spiral of the tree. The type I purchased—sold for general household use—featured a clear, pale green vinyl coating that was perfect for my holiday tree. Once you shape the coil, wrap it with a single strand of Christmas tree lights. I used pearl lights, which have small marble-sized bulbs, but any kind of minilights will look attractive. Fold the strand in half, and begin wrapping the folded end from the top of the tree.

The treetop is a lamp finial, which, in addition to being decorative, clamps the wire spiral securely to the trunk. You can substitute a curtain finial or a large glass bead to perform the same function. To finish, I concealed the plaster base with a scrap of white velvet (you could also use reindeer moss), and I hung soft pink antique glass ornaments. Choose the ornaments for your tree from your own collection.

A. Embed
a garden
stake
upside
down
in plaster.

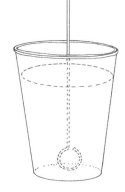

Materials

Makes one 30"-tall spiral tree

- 6" decorative container
- Strand of 35 pearl lights
- Assorted ornaments
- White velvet fabric scrap (for tree skirt)
- Lamp finial (or other topper)
- 28" single-loop garden stake
- 14-gauge green vinyl-coated steel wire
- 1-quart disposable container
- Plaster of Paris
- Florist clay

You'll also need:
Flat-nose pliers; wire cutter; tape measure; masking tape; wet and dry measuring cups; and spoon.

Making the Spiral Tree

1. **PREPARE BASE AND TRUNK.** Place 2 cups water in 1-quart disposable container. Add 4 cups dry plaster of Paris (or ratio that manufacturer recommends) and stir until dissolved. Set garden stake in container, loop end down. Crisscross strips of masking tape across container opening to hold stake upright and centered as plaster hardens. Let cure 30 minutes. Remove tape (illustration A).

2. **BEND SPIRAL.** Stand container inside coiled ring of 14-gauge wire. Using pliers, bend wire at right angle ¾" from end. Just above bend, cut through and remove plastic wrapping, exposing bare wire. Grasp bare wire and pull coil straight up around trunk. Bend wire in toward center of coil so that you can tape bare section to top of trunk (illustration B). To shape spiral, start at top and work down. Bend wire around trunk in open, airy spiral, making four or five revolutions that increase in size and spacing as you approach container rim. For a smooth, sinuous curve, bend short sections at a

B. Tape a wire coil
to the top of the
stake trunk.

time in small increments; you can always go back and fine-tune the shape later (illustration C). Clip wire from coil a few inches beyond where it touches container rim.

3. **ADD PEARL LIGHTS TO SPIRAL.** Untape wire spiral and remove it from trunk. Fold strand of pearl lights in half so each light has a partner and plug end extends about 12". Part light strand slightly at fold, and lodge bent tip of spiraled wire between them. Wind double strand of lights around spiral wire. Adjust spacing as needed so end of strand coincides with end of spiral (illustration D).

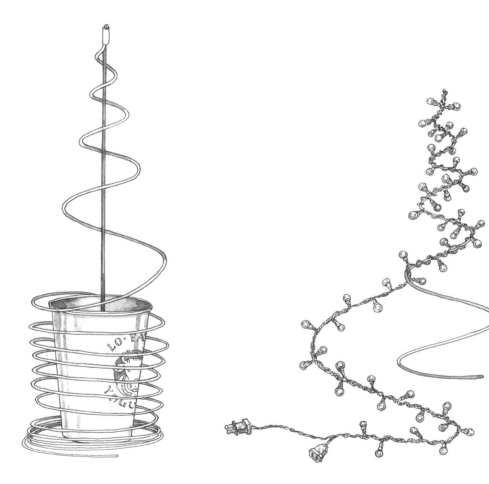

C. Shape the coil into a gentle spiral.

D. Remove the spiraled wire to add the light strand.

4. **REATTACH SPIRAL.** Fit spiral around trunk. At top, slip finial onto trunk, then push exposed spiral wire up into base of finial until snug. At bottom, tape end of spiraled wire to container rim, letting socket fall to inside of container (illustration E).

5. **TRIM THE TREE.** Conceal plaster container inside decorative container, stabilizing it with pieces of florist clay inserted at sides. Conceal top of plaster and socket with scrap of white velvet arranged as tree skirt. Hang ornaments from spiraled section, using strand of lights to keep hooks from slipping (illustration F). Plug in lights for the full effect.

Designer's Tips

• Change the look of your tree by the base you choose. Possibilities include terra cotta pots, brass planters, ceramic vases, and wine buckets. The tree should be approximately five times the pot height.

• Decorate your spiral tree in a special theme. For example, you may want to use the tree to showcase all your favorite miniature ornaments or combine different ornaments in a particular color scheme. Choose a light strand in a style to complement the ornaments you use.

E. Reattach the spiral
at the top and base.

F. Trim the finished tree
with miniature ornaments.

Boxwood Welcome Tree

Use live greens to make this front door topiary that looks like it was just cut from the forest.

by Dawn Anderson

GREET YOUR HOLIDAY VISITORS WITH THIS FRESH TREE-SHAPED TOPIARY, designed to lay flush against any door or wall. It's only ornamentation consists of wire-edged ribbon looped into a simple bow at the top, with tails that cascade down the sides. The result is a decoration that will last throughout the holiday season, welcoming your guests with its understated elegance.

The featured topiary is made with boxwood, but you can substitute other fresh evergreens. Purchase your greenery from a florist or local Christmas tree farm, or better yet, gather cuttings from your garden or a nearby woods, or use the extra branches trimmed from your Christmas tree. You can even mix different types of greenery for a more casual look, or add some holly sprigs with bright red berries for an additional festive touch.

To make the topiary base, glue foam sheets together with Hot-Glue Help Mate, which holds even in cold temperatures. And be sure to choose a color-fast, water-repellent ribbon that will stand up to the elements.

Materials

Makes one 30"-long door decoration

- 3 to 4 bunches fresh boxwood
- 10" x 10" x 4" flush-mount container
- Sheet moss
- 4 yards 2"-wide pink plaid wire-edged ribbon
- 2" x 12" x 36" foam sheet
- 18-gauge 18" florist wire stems
- 20-gauge 18" florist wire stems
- 30-gauge wire
- Florist pins
- Two 6" florist picks
- ¾" wood dowel
- Hold the Foam glue
- Hot-Glue Help Mate

You'll also need:
Tree form pattern (see page 53); hot-glue gun; wire cutter; small handsaw; serrated knife; pliers; pruning shears; tape measure; scissors; and spray mister.

Making the Topiary

1. **MAKE TREE FORM.** Lay pattern on foam sheet. Run serrated knife along pattern outline to score foam, then cut clear through. Repeat to cut second piece. Reserve excess foam. Following manufacturer's directions, use Hot-Glue Help Mate and hot glue to join pieces together to make one 4"-thick piece (illustration A). [Editor's note: Hot glue cools and holds immediately, while Hot-Glue Help Mate requires overnight drying time. You may proceed with project while Help Mate is drying, but keep

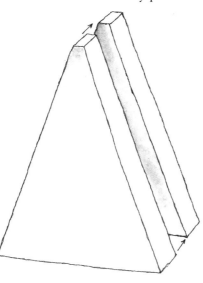

A. Glue the two foam pieces together.

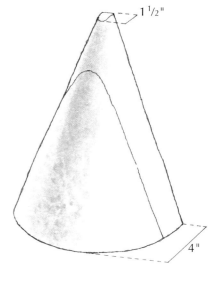

1 ½"

B. Shave the foam to make a half-cone shape.

4"

in mind that wet glue will ooze.] Using knife, shave off edges to create half-cone shape that is 4" thick at bottom center and tapers to 1½" thickness at peak (illustration B).

2. **COVER FORM WITH SHEET MOSS.** Lightly spray-mist sheet moss for easier handling. Open misted sheets, mist again, and set aside so moisture can seep in. Cut a dozen or so 3" to 6" lengths of 20-gauge wire stem. Using pliers, bend each wire into a hairpin shape and crinkle the ends. Push hairpin wires into foam form according to depth to help secure layers together. Layer sheet moss over form and secure with hot glue and hairpin wires. Continue until entire form, including flat back, is covered.

3. **ADD WIRE HANGER.** Bend 18-gauge wire stem at middle, twist to make 2" loop, then bend loop up 90 degrees. Insert free ends of wire into flat back of tree 5" below peak (illustration C). Push through until loop rests flush against moss. On front, twist ends together and bend up.

4. **FIT DOWEL STEM.** Cut excess foam to fit into flush-mount container. Pack tightly, and secure with extra-long handmade hairpins. Saw 14" length from ¾" dowel. Center dowel above container and push straight down into foam. To join tree, lay container and tree flat on work surface, center end of stem against base of tree, and push both pieces together until tree and container are flush (illustration D). Remove dowel from both pieces. Use Hold the Foam glue to secure dowel in container hole only.

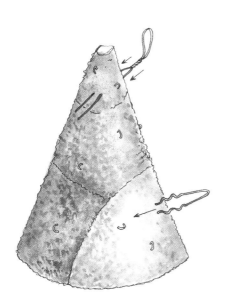

C. Attach sheet moss and add a wire hanger.

D. Test-fit the half-topiary on a flush-mount base.

5. **ATTACH BOXWOOD SPRIGS TO TREE.** Using pruning sheers, cut boxwood into 6" to 8" sprigs. Place one sprig at base of tree, leaves "growing" down and extending 1" to 1½" beyond lower edge. Secure with florist pins. Repeat process to conceal entire lower edge. Add second row of sprigs in same way, overlapping first row to conceal pins (illustration E). Strive for lush, full appearance rather than rigidly spaced rows. Continue until you reach top (pins will be concealed by bow). Also pin sprigs to underside of base, radiating out from center hole.

6. **ADD BOW WITH STREAMERS.** Refer to "Making a Six-Loop Bow" (facing page). Fold ribbon in half to locate middle. Observing midpoint, fold ribbon accordion-style to make six 8" loops. Crimp loops at middle, bind with 30-gauge wire, and clip off excess wire. To hide wire, wrap one ribbon streamer once around middle. Secure bow to top of tree by inserting wire hairpin around center of bow and through foam, twisting together at back, and clipping off excess. Fluff out bow loops, and trim ends of streamers with inverted V. Arrange streamers down each side of tree, securing cascades with florist pins (illustration F). Insert two 6" florist picks halfway into base foam on each side of dowel. Apply Hold the Foam glue to exposed dowel. Insert dowel in tree, pushing firmly. Let dry 24 hours.

E. Pin on boxwood sprigs layer by layer.

F. Add a ribbon and join the base permanently.

MAKING A SIX-LOOP BOW

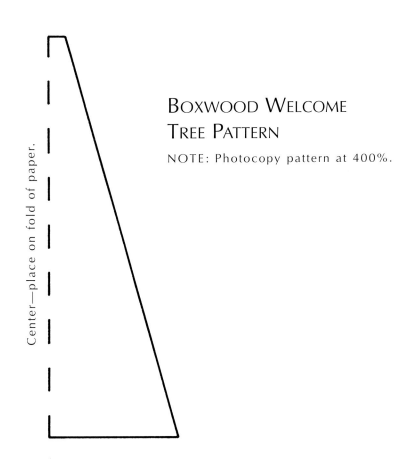

Center—place on fold of paper.

BOXWOOD WELCOME
TREE PATTERN

NOTE: Photocopy pattern at 400%.

Diamond Cherub Ornaments

Create Old English–style ornaments by combining stamped images, parchment paper, and gold accents.

by Dawn Anderson

Looking for a beautiful ornament idea? Consider these traditionally styled ornaments that look as if they are covered with antique sheet music.

The background design for the face of the diamond is made by creating a horizontal pattern with two rubber stamps. Though I used one stamp with a line of holiday text and another with a few bars of music, you could combine other stamp motifs to create your own antique-look paper. Just think of the background as a wallpaper with a repeating symmetrical design. I recommend testing the stamps and working out the spacing on plain paper before applying the designs to the parchment paper.

To add the final touches, glue a cherub to the center of the diamond and thread beads and a glittering tassel through the bottom point.

Materials

Makes one ornament

- 5"-long papier-mâché diamond ornament
- Medium-weight parchment paper
- Cherub charm (up to 2")
- 2" metallic gold tassel
- 10mm mesh-encased bead
- 2 gold seed beads
- Gold beading thread
- 2 ounces DecoArt metallic gold acrylic paint
- Gold pigment-based ink
- Clear embossing powder
- Yes Stikflat glue
- Multipurpose cement

You'll also need:
Two rubber stamps, such as (1) G-clef staff with notes or (2) "Peace at Christmas!" script; thin craft foam; embossing heat gun; X-Acto knife with new blade; self-healing cutting mat; quilter's grid ruler; soft brush (for paint); stiff brush (for glue); T-pin; beading needle; white paper; scissors; and pencil.

Making the Cherub Ornament

1. **EMBOSS PARCHMENT DIAMONDS.** Using papier-mâché diamond as a template, lightly trace two diamond outlines on parchment; allow ample margins. Apply gold ink to craft foam, then load either rubber stamp. With ruler as guideline, stamp horizontally across diamond, going out beyond edges. Immediately, while ink is still wet, sprinkle embossing powder within diamond outline. Shake off and reserve excess. Repeat process to stamp both diamonds with alternating lines (illustration A). To activate embossing powder, hold heat gun a few inches from parchment and heat until powder melts.

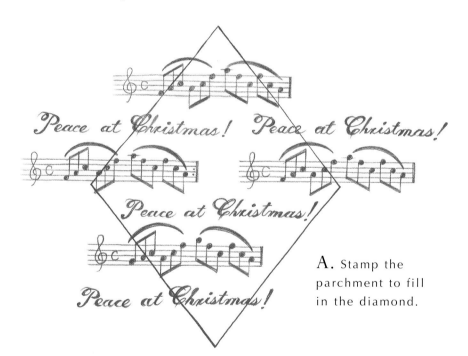

A. Stamp the parchment to fill in the diamond.

Designer's Tip

Try this stamping technique on the remnants of your parchment to create your own gift cards.

2. **ASSEMBLE DIAMONDS.** Paint sides and edges of papier-mâché diamond gold (do not paint interiors, which will be concealed by parchment diamonds). Let dry 20 minutes. Apply second coat if needed. Using X-Acto knife, grid ruler, and mat, cut out each parchment diamond ⅛" inside marked outline; use grid ruler to ensure that opposite edges are parallel. Turn parchment diamond facedown on white paper and brush thin coat of Yes glue across back and out beyond edges. Glue one parchment diamond to each side of papier-mâché diamond, pressing firmly to adhere (illustration B).

3. **ADD TRIMS.** Thread beading needle with 12" double strand of gold beading thread. String on seed bead, 10mm bead, and second seed bead. Push T-pin horizontally through bottom point of diamond to make two holes. Draw needle through both holes, go back down through beads in reverse order, and into tassel head. Repeat once more, going up through tassel head, through beads, through diamond, and back through beads (illustration C). Pull thread ends taut. Tie ends in square knot, draw knot down inside tassel head, and trim off tails. Use multipurpose cement to affix cherub charm to front of diamond.

B. Glue the parchment diamond to the painted ornament.

C. Join beads and a tassel to the lower point.

Gold Mesh Ornament

Envelop a simple glass ornament with gold mesh ribbon.

by Dawn Anderson

TRANSFORM ANY GLASS BALL ORNAMENT WITH A SIMPLE CORSET of gold mesh ribbon. The ribbon is sewn into a narrow sleeve that slips over the ball and is cinched at each pole. Both cinched ends are covered with delicate, decorative bead caps.

The featured ornament uses a glass ball with a satin finish, but you can substitute ornaments with a shiny or satin-thread finish. In fact, you can even use your much-loved faded or paint-worn glass ornaments; this gold mesh finish will disguise their tiny flaws.

Materials

Makes one 3" ornament

- 3" ball ornament with gold cap
- 2 matching 8mm glass beads
- 12" x 5½" -wide gold mesh ribbon
- Two ½" gold bead caps
- 20-gauge brass wire
- 2" head pin
- 2" eye pin
- Invisible nylon sewing thread
- Sewing thread
- Tacky glue

You'll also need:
Sewing machine (optional); round-nose pliers; chain-nose jewelry pliers; wire cutter; ½" dowel; scissors; ruler; hand-sewing needle; and pencil with eraser tip.

Making the Gold Mesh Ornament

1. **MAKE MESH SLEEVE.** Wrap mesh ribbon once around ball, allowing ½" overlap. Cut off excess. Remove wire, if any, from ribbon edges. Fold ribbon in half, cut edges matching. Using invisible thread, backstitch ¼" from cut edges (or sew by machine). Finger-press seam allowance to one side. Turn right side out.

2. **COVER BALL WITH MESH.** Ease sleeve onto 3" ball ornament with open ends at top and bottom. Remove ornament cap. Using invisible thread, hand-baste 1" from top edge once around. Pull thread ends to gather mesh around top of ball and tie off. Gently poke excess mesh into opening with eraser end of pencil (illustration A). Twist opposite end until mesh hugs ball, bind twisted section with thread, and tie off. Trim close to knot. Using invisible thread, backstitch around ornament neck to take up slack.

A. Sheathe a glass ball ornament with gold mesh.

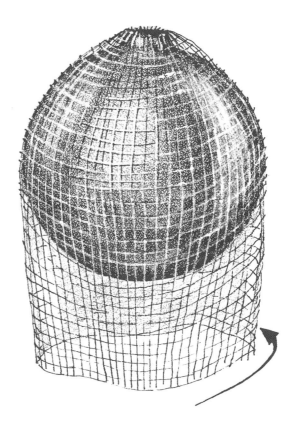

3. **ASSEMBLE CAP.** Remove wire from ornament cap and discard. Cut 4" length of brass wire. Using chain-nose pliers, make 90-degree bend at middle and again ⅜" away. Grip middle section with round-nose pliers, then bend each arm down to shape loop. Insert wire ends through bead cap and ornament cap. On underside, press wires against inside of bead cap. Bend wires at right angles to follow cap contours (illustration B). Reattach cap to ornament.

4. **ADD WIRE HANGER.** Cut 3½" length of brass wire. Using chain-nose pliers, make 90-degree bend ⅜" from one end. Using round-nose pliers, shape this short section into loop. Slip bead onto wire, then loop other end in same way. To shape hook, make 135-degree bend 1" above lower loop. Roll section above bend around dowel to shape hook. Open lower loop, slip through ornament-cap loop, and close.

5. **CAP BOTTOM.** Slide remaining bead onto head pin. Bend pin wire down 90 degrees, clip ⅜" from bend, and shape loop. Slip eye pin through bead cap, and clip and loop end. Join together loops on bead and bead cap. Glue bead cap over knot at bottom of ornament; secure top cap with glue if needed (illustration C).

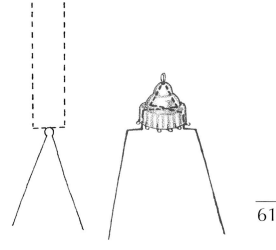

B. Bend wire to fit the ornamental caps.

61

C. Add a hook at the top, and cap the bottom.

Rhinestone Partridge and Pear

Pave artificial forms with clay and glittering stones.

by Dawn Anderson

RADIANT SOPHISTICATION CHARACTERIZES THIS PAIR OF KEEPSAKE tree ornaments. Fully encrusted with a colorful mix of rhinestones, this sparkling partridge and pear will surely be treasured as family heirlooms.

The ornaments are easy to make. The forms are first covered with a layer of clay and lightly sanded and painted to create a color guide; then matching rhinestones in corresponding colors are glued to each area. The tail feathers and crest of the partridge are made from short lengths of wire planted into the form and strung with beads.

The ornaments shown here were made from glass rhinestones, which will cost approximately $20 to $30 for each ornament. I thought this was reasonable, considering what one could spend for comparable glass or decorator ornaments at department stores. A less expensive alternative is to use acrylic rhinestones, which are about half the price; although the weight and feel of the ornament will be different, they will look practically the same on the tree. You can also substitute less expensive glass seed beads for the Austrian diamond-shaped crystal beads that are used on the crest and tail feathers.

Materials

Makes one partridge and pear ornament set

- 3"-long artificial bird
- 2½"-high plastic pear
- 6mm flat-backed rhinestones: approximately 300 topaz, 100 sapphire, 75 emerald, 15 ruby, 3 clear
- 4½mm rhinestones: approximately 300 topaz, 100 sapphire, 75 emerald, 15 ruby, 15 clear
- 2¾mm Austrian diamond-shaped crystal beads: 53 sapphire, 41 topaz
- 2 red 4mm glass bird eyes
- 2 gold bird leg clips
- Five 3" head pins
- Two 2" head pins
- 28-gauge brass craft wire
- 16-gauge brass craft wire
- One 2" velvet leaf
- Scrap of green cotton fabric
- 8 ounces Creative Paperclay
- 2-ounce Folk Art acrylic paints: Pure Metallic Gold, Blue Sapphire, Engine Red, Garnet Red, Shamrock, Emerald Green, Pearl White, Black
- White high-tack glue

You'll also need:
Jewelry pliers; round-nose pliers; wire cutter; awl; mini screwdriver; tweezers; 240-grit sandpaper; plastic paint palette; ½" flat paintbrush; ¼" round paintbrush; foam brick; spray mister; paper towels; scissors; and pencil.

Making the Partridge

1. **MAKE WIRE HOLDER.** Remove feathers and legs/feet, if any, from artificial bird. Cut 10" length of 16-gauge wire. Bend 2"-long portion into hairpin shape. Use awl to pierce two holes in bird's back and one in underbelly. Insert wire through holes so hairpin shape lodges in body and long end of wire exits through underbelly. Stand wire stem in foam brick to hold bird upright while you work.

2. **ADD HEAD PINS.** Pierce one hole at top center of head and two holes ¼" away on each side. Insert 2" head pin through each side hole and out top hole, and twist together once at top of head. Bend wires forward slightly. In same way, pierce five evenly spaced holes across base of tail feathers, about ¼" from edge. Pierce five corresponding holes along edge rim. Thread 3" head pin through each base hole and out of rim hole. Pull wires snug and bend up slightly (illustration A, facing page).

3. **COAT BIRD WITH CLAY.** Press and mold Creative Paperclay over entire bird body, making ³⁄₁₆" layer. Smooth with wet fingers; if air bubbles develop, break them open and resmooth. Let dry overnight. Sand to achieve extra-smooth finish. Wipe off dust with lightly misted paper towel (illustration B).

4. **PAINT BIRD.** Paint bird body metallic gold; let dry 20 minutes. Using pencil, sketch in lines to denote different color areas of bird's body. Paint wings green, back and chest blue, and throat white as indicated. Apply additional coats as needed for full coverage. Paint beak black (illustration C).

5. **GLUE RHINESTONES TO BIRD.** Clip wire that joins glass eyes, leaving each eye with ⅛" stem. Push each stem into gold area of head and glue in place. Glue small topaz rhinestones around each eye by applying dot of glue to bird and positioning rhinestone. Use tweezers to butt rhinestones together so gaps are as small as possible. Continue gluing stones until gold area of head is fully encrusted (illustration D).

    In same way, glue clear rhinestones to throat, sapphire stones to back and breast, emerald stones to wings, and gold stones to underbelly, matching rhinestone color to painted color. Intersperse large and small stones to fill in each color area without gaps.

6. **ADD BEADED PLUMAGE.** Separate head wires so one falls slightly forward. Thread 7 topaz and 2 sapphire crystal beads on front wire. Bend excess wire at 90-degree angle and clip, leaving ½" tail. Use round-nose pliers to coil tail into loop. Repeat process for second head wire, using 9 topaz and 2 sapphire beads. Treat tail wires in similar way: Starting with end wire, thread on 9 sapphire and 5 topaz beads. Bend up excess wire 90 degrees and coil in flat spiral. Continue in this fashion, using 10 sapphire beads on next wire and 11 sapphire beads on middle wire (illustration D). Bead remaining wires in mirror image so sapphire color flares out at middle.

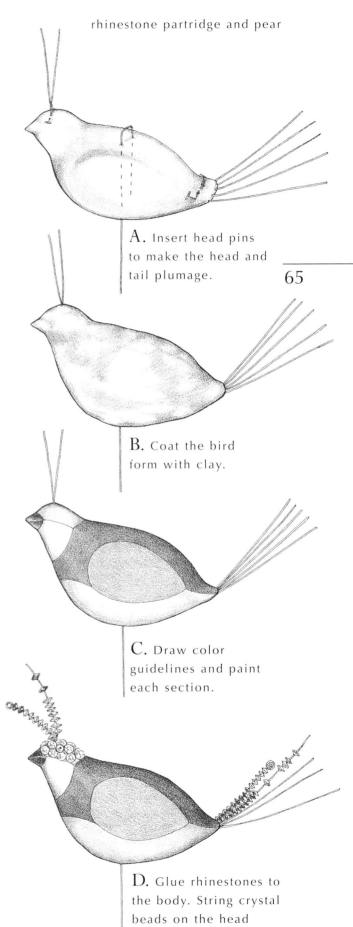

A. Insert head pins to make the head and tail plumage.

B. Coat the bird form with clay.

C. Draw color guidelines and paint each section.

D. Glue rhinestones to the body. String crystal beads on the head pins.

E. Add a clip holder at the bottom.

7. **ATTACH CLIP.** Using mini screwdriver, pry up prongs on top half of clip to release curved spring-clip mechanism. Set aside bottom half of clip. Slip coiled spring from clip onto wire stem of bird and slide it snug against bird's underbelly. Cut wire 7/8" beyond end of spring and bend it onto clip. To rejoin the two halves, set curved mechanism back in position. Reclamp prongs, securing wire stem underneath (illustration E).

Making the Pear

1. **MAKE WIRE HOLDER.** Remove pear stem and leaf if any. Attach wire as described in partridge, step 1, making sure the long wire emerges from the stem hole.
2. **COAT PEAR WITH CLAY.** Use same technique as described in partridge, step 3 (illustration F).
3. **PAINT PEAR.** Paint pear metallic gold; let dry 20 minutes. Mix 1 part Garnet Red and 1 part Engine Red to paint red oval blush on pear surface. Apply additional coats as needed for even coverage.
4. **GLUE RHINESTONES TO PEAR.** Glue topaz and ruby rhinestones to pear, using technique described in partridge, step 5 (illustration G).

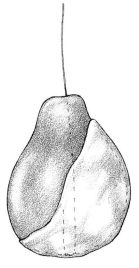

F. Coat a plastic pear with clay.

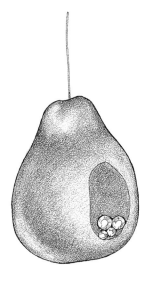

G. Paint the pear, and glue on colored rhinestones.

5. **MAKE LEAF.** Remove stem from velvet leaf. Use leaf as template to cut same shape from green cotton fabric. Cut 9" length of 28-gauge wire. Glue leaves back to back, sandwiching wire in between for a stem. Glue emerald rhinestones to one side of leaf (illustration H). Let dry 30 minutes. Glue rhinestones to other side.

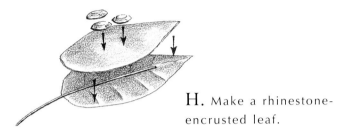

H. Make a rhinestone-encrusted leaf.

6. **ATTACH CLIP AND LEAF.** Attach clip to pear at stem location, using same technique as for partridge, step 7. Coil wire leaf stem neatly around spring and clip off excess (illustration I).

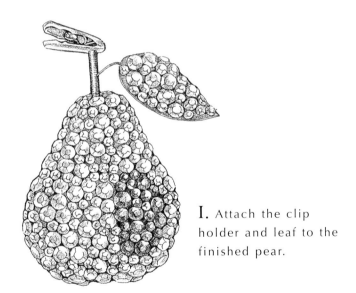

I. Attach the clip holder and leaf to the finished pear.

Beaded Window Icicles

Use an easy double-back technique to turn crystal beads into a wintry window accent.

by Elizabeth Cameron

THESE CASCADING STREAMS OF CRYSTAL BEADS CONJURE UP images of icicles dripping in the sunlight. They even twinkle in the glow of evening lights.

The construction technique is so simple that no beading experience is necessary. Simply run a wire through a bead as if you were stringing a necklace, and then, before you string the next bead, double back, looping the wire around the outside of the first bead and back through it again, trapping it in place.

Create your beaded strands in various lengths to imitate the uneven formation of real icicles. To suggest the shapes of melting icicles, you can string smaller beads at the bottom of the strand and increasingly larger beads as you work your way up.

Once the strands are complete, staple them to a lightweight basswood strip, then attach the strip to the window with a putty adhesive. The length of the basswood strip and the length of the icicles are very adaptable. For instance, if draperies hide part of your window, you can string beads to fill the space between them. When spring arrives, you can easily peel away your winter decorations.

Materials

Fits window 24" to 30" wide

- 250 to 350 assorted crystal beads
- 32-gauge silver wire
- $\frac{1}{2}$" x $\frac{3}{8}$" x 30" basswood strip
- Putty adhesive (such as FunTak)
- Paint to match window frame

You'll also need:
Staple gun with $\frac{5}{16}$" staples; round-nose pliers; flat-nose pliers; wire cutters; small saw; sandpaper; small, flat brush; and tape measure.

Making the Icicles

1. **CUT WIRE.** Cut basswood strip to fit window frame. Measure down from mounting location to determine longest icicle drop and cut one wire double this length. Determine length of shortest icicle drop and cut one wire double this length. Snip various lengths in between these two until you have one wire for every inch of basswood strip.

2. **STRING BOTTOM BEAD.** Select one precut wire strand. Insert wire into bead with wire extending 2". Bring end of wire around bead and reinsert it through same hole. Pull wire ends tight, trapping bead in loop. Bend short end 90 degrees and clip, leaving $\frac{3}{8}$" tail (illustration A). Use round-nose pliers to shape tail into loop.

A. Loop the wire to secure the bottom bead.

3. **STRING SUCCEEDING BEADS.** Slide new bead onto wire, stopping ¼" to 1" above bottom bead. Draw working end of wire around bead and through hole from bottom to top. Pull snug, trapping bead in loop (illustration B). Repeat stringing and trapping motion to string beads to desired length. Repeat steps 2 and 3 for each precut strand.

B. Use the same technique to add each new bead.

4. **MOUNT BEADED STRANDS.** Paint basswood strip to match window frame; let dry. Lay strip flat, with ½"-wide surface face up. Arrange beaded strands in desired order. Using pliers, crimp excess wire at top of each strand into zigzag no wider than strip. Clip off any excess. Staple each zigzag section to strip, spacing strands at 1" intervals (illustration C). To mount, apply putty adhesive to back of strip at 6" intervals and press onto window frame.

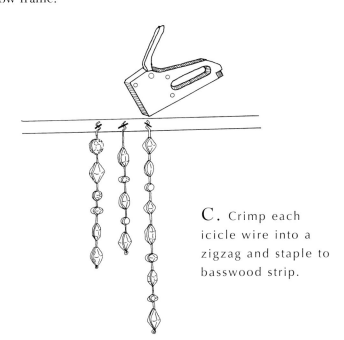

C. Crimp each icicle wire into a zigzag and staple to basswood strip.

Diamond Wreath with Kissing Ball

Use fresh boxwood and hot pink celosia to create a contemporary holiday wreath.

by Dawn Anderson

FOR A GRAPHIC TWIST ON THIS YEAR'S HOLIDAY WREATH, TRY AN angled shape—in this case a diamond—instead of the traditional circle. When I couldn't find a diamond wreath form, I simply shaped a square base into a diamond by pulling on two opposite corners until it elongated.

The greenery on my diamond wreath is boxwood, a hardy choice that will last for several weeks and dry to a soft green color. Celosia, known also as cockscomb because its broad flowers resemble the comb of a cock, is used to cover a kissing ball suspended from the apex of the diamond. The construction of the wreath is simple: Wrap small bundles of boxwood sprigs with wire, then bind them to the wreath form. The base of the kissing ball is a globe-shaped piece of foam that has been cut in half so that it will rest flat against the hanging surface. The foam has a base layer of moss and a top layer of celosia secured with hot glue and wire.

If you plan to hang your wreath on an outside door, be sure to weatherize it. Cold temperatures can weaken the bond of hot glue by causing the joins to become extremely brittle and break apart. A product called Hot-Glue Help Mate, applied at the same time as hot glue, will continue holding even when temperatures drop. Using hairpin-shaped wires in addition to glue will also stabilize the layer of celosia against the core. Sunlight can cause materials to fade so you may want to hang your wreath in a slightly shaded location like a porch or protected entryway. You might also consider spraying the celosia with Design Master color tool in raspberry to maintain its bright color. Select a ribbon that is colorfast and water-resistant so it will stand up to sunlight, snow, and rain.

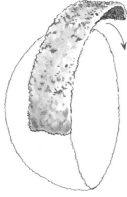

A. Cover a foam half-sphere with sheet moss.

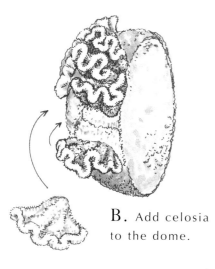

B. Add celosia to the dome.

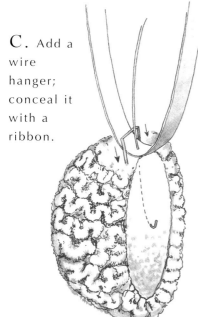

C. Add a wire hanger; conceal it with a ribbon.

Materials

Makes one 24" x 30" diamond wreath

- 4 to 5 bunches fresh boxwood
- 2 bunches hot pink celosia (cockscomb)
- Sheet moss
- Hot pink satin ribbon with gold edging from MOKUBA:
  1 yard ⅝"-wide
  2½ yards 1½"-wide
- Hot pink wire-edged organza ribbon: 2½ yards 4"-wide
- 16"-square wire wreath form
- 3" foam ball
- 18-gauge 18" florist wire stems
- 20-gauge 18" florist wire stems
- 22-gauge paddle wire
- 30-gauge paddle wire
- Green florist tape
- Design Master color spray (optional)

You'll also need:
Hot-glue gun; needle-nose pliers; wire cutter; pruning shears; serrated knife; scissors; and spray mister.

Making the Kissing Ball

1. **GLUE MOSS LAYER.** Using serrated knife, cut foam ball in half; set aside one-half for another project. Lightly spray-mist sheet moss for easier handling and less crumbling. Hot-glue sheet moss to remaining half-sphere, including flat cut surface (illustration A).
2. **ATTACH CELOSIA LAYER.** Cut two 20-gauge florist stems into 2" lengths. Using pliers, bend each wire into hairpin shape and crinkle the ends. Break celosia into small pieces. Secure celosia pieces to dome area of half-sphere using wire hairpins and hot glue. Leave moss on flat back exposed (illustration B). For nonfading color, apply floral color spray to dome, following manufacturer's instructions.
3. **ATTACH SUSPENDING WIRE.** Bend 18-gauge wire stem 1½" from one end to make hairpin shape. Push longer wire end into center back of kissing ball, angling it to exit through dome ½" from edge. Pull snug to anchor hairpin at center back. Fold ⅝" pink ribbon in half, pierce small hole at fold with tip of wire, and slide ribbon down to kissing ball. Cut 5" length of 18-gauge wire. Using pliers, bend wire into a staple equal to ribbon width. Push staple into kissing ball to anchor ribbon in place (illustration C).

Assembling the Wreath

1. **MAKE DIAMOND WREATH FORM.** Grip two opposite corners of wreath form and pull apart, distorting square into a diamond 26" long and 18" wide. Bind diamond-shaped form with florist tape, stretching tape slightly as you go.

2. **BIND BOXWOOD TO WREATH FORM.** Using pruning shears, clip boxwood into 6" to 8" sprigs. Hold 6 to 8 sprigs together and bind stems with 22-gauge paddle wire. Repeat process to make about 40 bundles. Hold one bundle against lower wreath form so leaves "grow" down, concealing diamond point. Bind bundle to wreath form with 22-gauge paddle wire; do not clip wire (illustration D). Position second bundle about 1" above first bundle, concealing its binding; bind in place. Continue binding bundles up one side of form to create full, lush foliage; keep back flat for flush mounting. Stop when you reach top. Repeat process on other side (illustration E). Wire one more bundle to top center, so bound stems extend slightly above point.

3. **SUSPEND KISSING BALL.** For hanger, bend an 18-gauge wire stem in half and twist to form 1" loop. Hold loop flat against wreath behind apex of diamond. Wrap wire ends several times around frame, twist ends together securely, and clip off excess. Wrap kissing ball wire around base of loop so ball is suspended in middle of diamond. Draw loose ribbons up to conceal suspending wire and bind ends to hanging loop with 22-gauge paddle wire.

4. **ADD BOW WITH STREAMERS.** Lay organza ribbon flat on work surface, layer 1½" satin ribbon on top, and locate middle. Observing midpoint and keeping satin ribbon on outside, make two continuous loops, each 14" long. Crimp at middle, bind with 30-gauge wire, and clip off excess. To hide wire, wrap one layered ribbon streamer once around middle. Wire ribbon to top of wreath, allowing tails to hang free (illustration F).

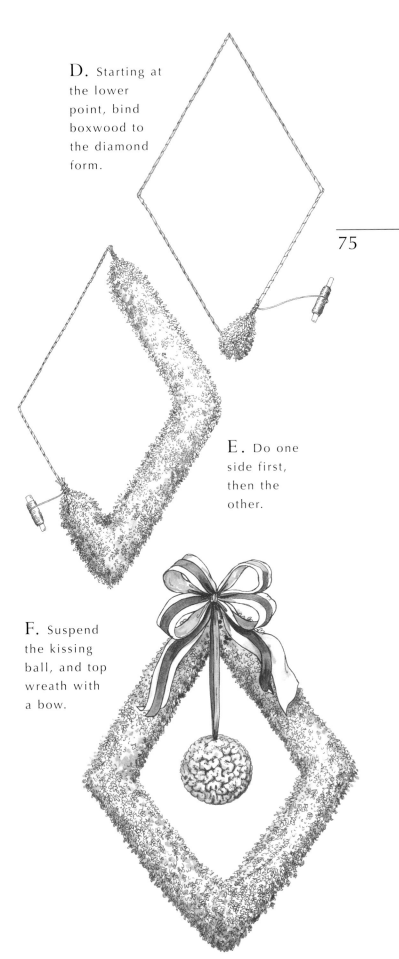

D. Starting at the lower point, bind boxwood to the diamond form.

E. Do one side first, then the other.

F. Suspend the kissing ball, and top wreath with a bow.

Heirloom Angel Tree Topper

This elegant tree topper requires ordinary craft materials and practically no sewing.

by Francoise Hardy

THOUGH THIS BEAUTIFUL ANGEL TREE TOPPER RESEMBLES A DOLL, with its porcelain face and draped robes, the construction is actually much simpler. The angel's body consists of a chipboard torso, which is stapled to a cone formed from posterboard. The angel's clothing, fashioned from paper, fabric, and assorted trims, is simply hot-glued to the cone. Finishing details include wings cut from chipboard, a rose and pearl veil, and metal charms at the waistband.

I started with a ready-made porcelain doll's head and hand set, purchased for $4.99. I needed to anchor the ceramic head to a torso of some type, to which the other parts of the angel could be attached. To make the torso, I used a thin piece of chipboard folded over and stapled at one end; the folded end is then glued into the curved base of the head unit. To make the lower half of the angel's body, I formed a cone from posterboard, which I stapled to the torso. The open underside of the cone will fit on top of a Christmas tree, while the angel's clothing can be attached on the outside. The clothing includes a moiré lining, a paper dress, and a fabric tunic, all of which are bound in place by a finishing waistband.

To make this angel as realistic as possible, it needed wings. I couldn't find pre-made wings that fit the style of the tree topper, so I cut my own from cardboard, then used acrylic gesso and fabric paint to add dimension. Then, I painted the wings gold and covered them with glitter. To attach the wings to the angel, I designed them with a tab, which is tucked into the back of the waistband.

Materials

Makes one tree topper, approximately 11" tall

♦ 3" porcelain doll's head and hand set
♦ ⅝ yard 45"-wide burgundy rayon velvet
♦ ¼ yard 45"-wide cream crinkle moiré
♦ 1 yard ⅜"-wide purple grosgrain ribbon
♦ Burgundy sewing thread
♦ 17" x 17" posterboard
♦ 14" x 14" 1-ply chipboard
♦ Thin kraft paper (on roll)
♦ Three 12" chenille stems
♦ 24-gauge brass wire
♦ 2 cotton balls
♦ Masking tape
♦ Pale gold micro glitter
♦ 2-ounce container blue acrylic paint
♦ 2-ounce container dark gold metallic acrylic paint
♦ Fabric paint (any color) in applicator bottle (e.g., Tulip Colorpoint)
♦ Acrylic gesso
♦ Acrylic gel medium
♦ White craft glue (e.g., Sobo)
♦ Acrylic spray sealer, matte finish

Trims
♦ 6" square green-gold sheer fabric (cut on selvage)
♦ 7½" square olive chiffon fabric
♦ ¼ yard 1½"-wide gold woven ribbon
♦ ⅔ yard ⅝"-wide brown wire-edged ribbon
♦ Five ½" pale pink ribbon roses
♦ ½ yard 4mm plastic pearls
♦ 6½"-long goldtone chain (e.g., cut from costume jewelry)
♦ Three 1" to 1½" goldtone key and cross charms
♦ 3 gold jump rings

You'll also need:
Torso, wing, and coat patterns (see pages 86–87); spray adhesive; X-Acto knife; acrylic grid ruler; self-healing cutting mat; large compass; protractor; soft (#1) pencil; metallic gold fine-tip marker; scissors; paper clamp; staple remover; stapler; chain-nose pliers; wire cutters; hot-glue gun; emery board; sewing machine; pins; sewing shears; clean, large soft-bristled brush; 1" flat bristle brush; medium round brush; detail brush; spray mister; copier paper; newsprint; and tall, narrow-necked bottle.

Getting Started

1. **Cut chipboard pieces.** Photocopy torso, wing, and coat patterns (pages 86–87); set coat pattern aside. Spray torso pattern with adhesive; affix pattern to 1-ply chipboard. Using X-Acto knife, acrylic grid ruler, and mat, cut along solid outline. To create smooth curve when bending torso later, score dash lines lightly. Set torso aside. Repeat process to cut wings, but do not score dash lines. Lift wing pattern from chipboard, reposition on new piece of chipboard, and cut separate blade for each wing. Lift off wing pattern and set aside.

2. **Cut fabric coat and dress pieces.** From burgundy velvet, cut one coat on fold, observing grain line. Open coat and lay it flat to cut front opening at one end as indicated on pattern; set cutout strip aside. From cream moiré, cut two 4"-square undersleeves, one 3"-square bodice, and one 7" x 10" skirt with crinkle grain running parallel to shorter edge.

3. **Cut paper gown pieces.** Cut 26" square of thin kraft paper. Mist both sides lightly until damp, gather softened paper into bundle, and twist gently to make "rope." Clamp ends together, and let dry overnight. Gently unfurl crimped rope, and lay it flat until bone-dry. Using acrylic grid ruler and pencil, draft one 10" x 24" skirt. Then draft two 5" x 8" arms with crinkle grain running parallel to shorter edge. Cut out pieces with scissors.

Making the Wings

NOTE: Insert wing tab into bottle to hold wings upright.

1. **Shape and seal wings.** Apply white craft glue to blades, position blades on front wings, and press to adhere; let dry 20 minutes. Lightly mist peaks and lower tips of wings on both sides. When chipboard is softened and pliable (1 to 2 minutes), carefully bend peaks forward and curve lower tips back (illustration A). To set curves, use 1" flat brush to apply heavy coat of acrylic gesso over entire wing surface; coat front and back of wings, but leave middle tab section plain; let dry 20 minutes. To soften and sculpt blade area, use 1" flat brush to apply acrylic gel up against blade so it lodges against ridge. To round off top edge, scrape brush along edge to deposit bead of gel, then run brush lightly along bead to smooth it. When gel is dry (1 to 4 hours), sand and round off edges with emery board.

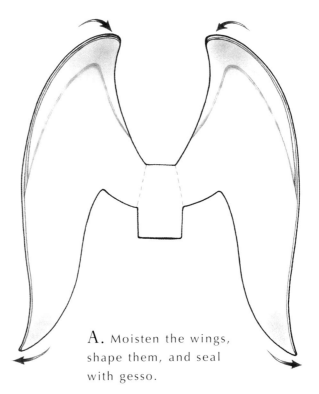

A. Moisten the wings, shape them, and seal with gesso.

2. **ADD FEATHER DETAILS AND GLITTER.** Lay wings faceup on flat surface. Referring to pattern, sketch in feather details lightly with soft pencil. To give feathers dimension, go over all sketched lines with fabric paint applied directly through fine-tipped nozzle. Let dry 1 hour, or until paint forms firm skin. Paint front and back of wings with gold acrylic paint; let dry 20 minutes. Brush very thin coat of white glue onto front and back of wings; do not coat middle tab section. Sprinkle pale gold micro glitter onto wings, catching excess on sheet of paper placed underneath (illustration B). Let dry 1 hour. Using clean, large soft-bristled brush, gently dust off loose glitter particles. Funnel excess glitter back into container. To prevent further shedding, spray wings with one or two light coats of acrylic matte sealer.

3. **PREPARE WINGS FOR JOINING TO ANGEL.** Rest wings faceup. Carefully score two center lines as indicated on pattern. Bend wings back slightly; final position can be adjusted after wings are attached to angel. Cut 3" length from reserved burgundy strip. Rest wings facedown. Hot-glue strip to wing tab and center section; curl side edges under and fold excess at top onto wing front and glue down (illustration C). Set wings aside.

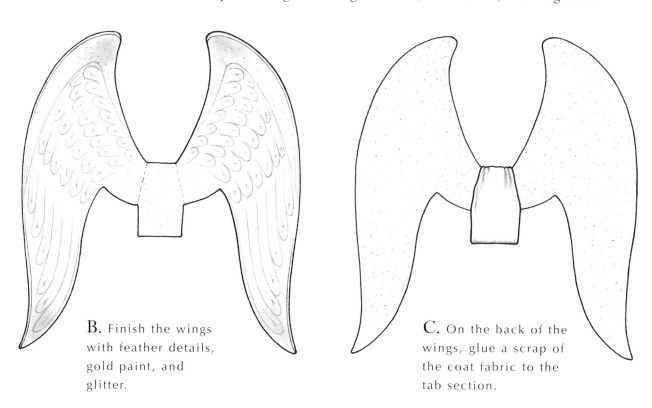

B. Finish the wings with feather details, gold paint, and glitter.

C. On the back of the wings, glue a scrap of the coat fabric to the tab section.

Making the Armature

1. **JOIN ANGEL HEAD TO TORSO.** Bend torso into U shape, score lines on inside, and staple bottom straight edges together. Apply hot glue generously to top curved section of torso. Set angel head on torso.

2. **JOIN TORSO TO CONE BASE.** Using compass, draft 16" circle on posterboard. Using protractor and acrylic grid ruler, draft 110-degree segment of circle. Cut out segment with scissors. To make base, curl segment into cone, overlapping straight edges ½" at bottom and tapering toward tip. Mark outside edge of overlap with pencil. Hot-glue overlapped sections together, then reinforce seam with tape. Remove staples from torso. Press pointed end of cone flat, fit torso over it, and staple through all layers (illustration D).

3. **ADD CHENILLE ARM PIECE TO TORSO.** Using 24-gauge wire, bind three chenille stems together at one end. Braid stems together, then bind other end; braid will be 10" to 11" long. For arm padding, cut 8" x 9" rectangle from kraft paper. Make ¼" accordion folds parallel to 8" edge, then bundle crinkled paper around braided arm piece to soften folds; to hold in place, crimp at middle and secure with dab of hot glue. Center arm piece inside torso loop and hot-glue to upper shoulders. Hot-glue porcelain hand to each end (illustration E).

D. Join the head and torso to a cone base.

E. Add chenille stem arms with paper-padded shoulders.

Adding the Clothes

1. **MAKE UNDERSLEEVES.** Roll one 4"-square undersleeve wrong side out to form loose tube; run crinkle grain along length of tube. Slide tube onto forearm, gather and crimp end around forearm/braided arm join, and bind with wire; remainder of tube will flow forward, covering hands. To shape billowing undersleeves, draw tube back on itself, turning it right side out. Gather and crimp end over previous join and bind with wire. Repeat process to make second sleeve.

2. **MAKE BODICE.** Lay cream bodice right side up, crinkle grain running vertically. Run bead of hot glue along lower edge. Quickly turn bodice facedown and press glue edge against lower edge of porcelain bust; bodice will cover face. Place two cotton balls on torso (illustration F). Fold bodice down over cotton balls and glue down side and bottom edges.

3. **MAKE UNDERSKIRT.** Lay cream skirt facedown on flat surface, with short edges at sides. Beginning at middle of top edge, shirr and crumple fabric with fingers. Set crumpled section against front lower edge of cone base, right side facing down, and secure with hot glue. Repeat process to glue fabric at each side (illustration G), swathing fabric around three-fourths of cone; leave back uncovered (it will be covered later). To cover cone, bring free edge up, and gather and crimp around waist, forming full, loose folds. Bind at waist with wire (illustration H, facing page).

82

F. Glue a fabric bodice to the bust section.

G. Crimp and glue the underskirt to the bottom of the cone.

4. **PAINT GOWN SKIRT AND SLEEVES.** Lay 10" x 24" paper gown skirt and 5" x 8" arms flat. Fold up one long edge of each piece ½". Cut 24-gauge wire 2" longer than folded edge. Set wire into crease, then glue down fold with white craft glue, encasing wire inside. Let dry 30 minutes, then clip off wire ends. Lay pieces flat on newsprint, hemmed side facedown. Using 1" brush, paint facing surface (right side) with blue acrylic paint; let dry 30 minutes. Using metallic gold fine-tip marker, draw cross-shaped stars interspersed with small dots in grid pattern across surface. Turn pieces over and paint reverse side dark gold metallic.

5. **ATTACH BLUE GOWN.** Gather blue skirt around torso waist, placing hemmed edge at bottom and overlapping edges at center front. If skirt is too long, trim waist edge with scissors. Bind skirt to waist with wire. Slip sleeves over arms and bind near bust/arm join; do not trim sleeves, as excess will be drawn up with ribbon garters. Secure all joins with hot glue. Part blue skirt in front to reveal cream skirt (illustration I).

6. **MAKE BURGUNDY VELVET COAT.** Fold coat in half, right side in, and machine-stitch side seams from lower edge to dots on pattern; finger-press seams open. Hot-glue ⅜"-wide purple ribbon to raw edges, mitering corners as indicated on pattern. Place coat on angel so lapels are ¾" to 1" apart, exposing bodice (illustration J, page 84).

83

H. Fold the skirt up and bind it at the waist.

I. Bind on the paper skirt and sleeves.

Assembling the Angel

1. **ADD WINGS AND GIRDLE.** Bind waist with wire, cinching coat into soft folds. Insert wing tab under wires at center back, so feathered side of wings faces front; secure with hot glue (illustration K). Hot-glue one end of 6½" chain to front waist, other end to back waist, so chain arcs across side skirt. Join key and cross charms to chain with jump rings. For girdle, cut 7½" length of 1½"-wide gold ribbon and 7½" square of olive chiffon. Cinch chiffon to form loose rope, center rope on ribbon, and wrap both around waist; secure with hot glue at center back. Shape wire-edged hem of blue skirt into soft, billowing folds. Arrange coat over blue skirt and secure at several spots with hot glue (illustration L).

2. **ADD ARMBANDS.** For each sleeve, cut 12" length of ⅝"-wide brown wire-edged ribbon. Tie ribbon snugly around sleeve above elbow, cinching concealed paper bundle; trim excess. Hot-glue strand of pearls to top of ribbon, trimming excess after coming full circle. Adjust paper sleeve to flare out over undersleeve, exposing gold lining (illustration L).

3. **ADD VEIL.** Drape 6"-square of green-gold sheer fabric on head so selvage falls loosely across crown; hot-glue at center and at back; turn raw edges under, and tuck remainder between wings and coat back. Dot back of pink ribbon rose with hot glue and press onto front edge of veil; glue will bleed through veil and adhere to hair. Attach four more roses in same way, framing face (illustration L). Cut 7" strand of pearls. Hot-glue ends to top center of crown to form circle; let remainder drape down back of veil.

J. Sew a simple coat from velvet.

K. Cinch the waist with wire to attach the wings.

Designer's Tip

Porcelain's inherent coolness causes hot glue to "freeze" quickly. To join porcelain pieces, apply hot glue to the nonporcelain component. To join the angel head, for example, apply the glue to the chipboard torso, not the porcelain head itself.

L. Finish with a girdle, veil, and other trims.

HEIRLOOM
ANGEL
TREE
TOPPER
PATTERNS

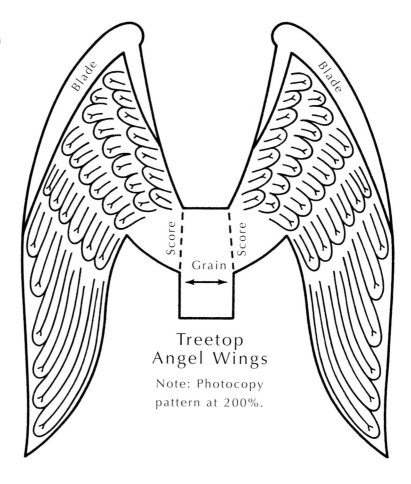

Blade   Blade

Score   Score

Grain

Treetop
Angel Wings

Note: Photocopy
pattern at 200%.

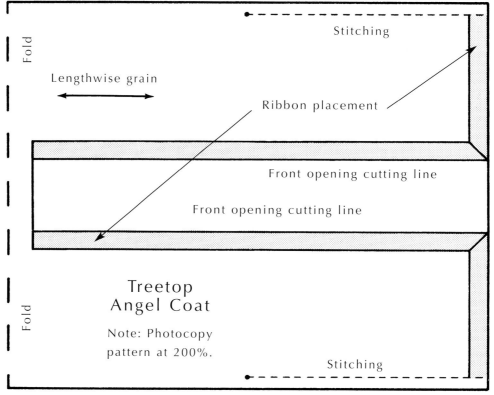

Fold

Stitching

Lengthwise grain

Ribbon placement

Front opening cutting line

Front opening cutting line

Treetop
Angel Coat

Note: Photocopy
pattern at 200%.

Fold

Stitching

HEIRLOOM
ANGEL
TREE
TOPPER
PATTERNS

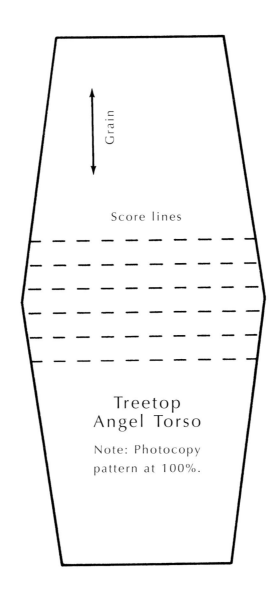

Grain

Score lines

Treetop
Angel Torso

Note: Photocopy
pattern at 100%.

Block-Print Gift Wrap

Block printing is still one of the best printing techniques around.

by Laura McFadden

Unique gift wraps can be made by block printing just about any type of sturdy paper. As in stenciling, a single design is repeated many times over—for lots of graphic punch with minimal effort.

If you did any block printing in art class, you may recall struggling to carve a design into a thin, hard layer of linoleum mounted on particle board. For this project, I chose a two-sided printing block instead. This block, about ⅜" thick, is flexible and rubbery, like a plastic eraser; a traditional linoleum cutting tool practically glides through the soft material. Don't concern yourself with flaws or nicks in your cutting. They will add a desirable handcrafted quirkiness to your prints.

While cutting the block is not physically hard, it is easy to confuse the positive and negative spaces in a design. I suggest working with the pattern on page 91 to get a feel for how a simple drawing translates into a cut block before going on to your own designs. Keep in mind that the cut line will always be thicker and bolder than the drawn design line and that the areas you cut away are the areas that won't print. If you like this technique, you might want to design one special block each year to print your holiday gift wrap. You can also create designs suitable for other occasions.

Materials

For assorted gift wraps:

♦ Colored paper (large sheets or roll)
♦ Speedball water-based block-printing inks

You'll also need:

Pattern (page 91); Speedball 9" x 12" Speedy Cut two-sided printing block, linoleum cutter handle with medium-sized blade, and 4" rubber brayer; 9" x 12" Plexiglas; ½" painter's tape; palette knife; tracing paper; graphite powder; sharp pencil; utility knife; and drying line.

Making the Gift Wrap

1. **TRANSFER THE DESIGN.** Photocopy the pattern on page 91. Turn pattern over and lightly dust reverse side with graphite powder. Position pattern, graphite side down, on Speedy Cut block, and tape in place. Using sharp pencil, trace over all lines to transfer design to block (illustration A).

2. **CUT THE PRINTING BLOCK.** With linoleum cutter, cut along all solid design lines, making grooves about ⅛" deep (illustration B). Cut a second line about ¼" from the design line; then cut away background around reindeer outline, carving about ⅛" deep.

A. Transfer design.

B. Cut along solid lines with a linoleum cutter.

3. **PREPARE THE INK PALETTE.** Lay colored paper on large flat work surface and tape down edges. Squeeze some printing ink from tube onto Plexiglas sheet, add a few drops of water, and mix thoroughly with palette knife. Roll brayer across ink to load it, then roll even coat of ink onto printing block. Set block, ink side down, on lower left corner of paper, then pound with your fist to ensure complete contact with paper. Pull up block to reveal print. Reload brayer and repeat, printing designs from left to right across paper until entire surface is covered (illustration C). Line-dry printed paper for 1 hour.

C. Load ink onto stamp with brayer; then turn block, ink side down, onto paper and pound with fist to make impression

REINDEER PATTERN FOR GIFT WRAP
Note: Photocopy to the size you prefer.

Lantern Gift Card

Use a rubber-stamped vellum window and a gilded interior to create a card that opens into a votive candle screen.

by Carol Endler Sterbenz

IF YOU'RE LOOKING FOR A SMALL GIFT FOR SOMEONE SPECIAL, tuck this miniature card under a napkin on your holiday table or attach it to the ribbon of a gift box. Made from cardstock and a scrap of vellum, the folded card opens into a small box-style lantern, perfectly sized to house a standard votive candle. The recipient peels up a star sticker found on an inside flap and uses it to secure the screen in its display position. The gilded interior reflects the candle's glowing light, a process made simple by using spray adhesive to adhere the leaf.

You will need to cut a window in one panel of the card to accommodate the vellum through which the candlelight shines. The fun part of this project is choosing the silhouette image to fit this space. I used a rubber stamp depicting a cozy house, but there are numerous other possibilities. You could use small graphic images like stars, pine cones, or holly leaves, or to personalize the card, you could use initials to create a lighted monogram or spell out a longer greeting like JOY or PEACE. The stamped image is enhanced with embossing powder, which adds a textural accent and shines even when the candle isn't lit.

Materials

Makes two cards with envelopes

- 11" x 17" red cardstock
- Scrap of vellum
- Composition gold leaf
- Four ½" self-adhesive gold stars
- Gold embossing powder
- Yellow stamp pad ink
- Invisible tape
- Yes Stikflat glue
- Spray adhesive

You'll also need:
Envelope pattern (page 96); gold metallic pen; holiday theme rubber stamp, image not to exceed 1½" x 2"; toaster (or embossing heat gun); X-Acto knife; quilter's acrylic grid ruler; self-healing cutting mat; thin craft foam; small flat brush; butter knife; heavy book; pencil; newsprint; cotton balls; and T-pin.

Making the Card

NOTE: Complete each step twice to make two cards with envelopes.

1. **Cut and fold card.** Using X-Acto knife, grid ruler, and mat, cut 3" x 11" rectangle from red cardstock. Fold in one end about ½" and crease well to make flap. Bring folded edge to opposite cut edge, crease at middle, and open (illustration A). Bring cut edge almost to middle crease, crease well, and open. Repeat from folded edge. Side facing up is inside of card.

A. Start by making two folds.

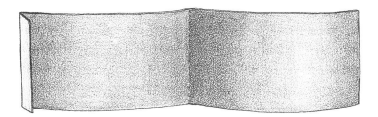

2. **Cut window opening.** Cut 2½" x 3" panel from red cardstock. Draft lines ½" in from each edge. Cut on marked lines to make 1½" x 2" window opening. Counting from flap, position panel on second card panel. Trace window opening on card and cut out (illustration B).

B. Fold four panels total, then cut a window opening.

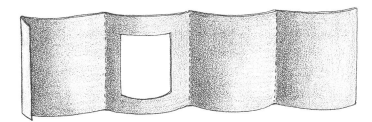

3. **Gild card and window panel.** Transfer two sheets of gold leaf to newsprint, placing them end to end. Lay card flat, inside faceup, on separate newsprint. Apply spray adhesive, following manufacturer's instructions. As soon as card surface is tacky with no wet spots (15 seconds or less), press card, adhesive side down, on gold leaf and rub gently to adhere. Turn card over and press gently with cotton ball. Use leaf remnants to gild remaining bare spots. Gild separate window panel with leaf remnants in same way. Let dry 30 minutes to 1 hour. Buff edges with cotton ball to remove skewings.

4. **CREATE WINDOW INSERT.** Brush yellow ink on craft foam. Load rubber stamp with ink, and stamp image on vellum. Immediately, while ink is still wet, sprinkle with embossing powder. Shake off and reserve excess. To activate embossing powder, hold vellum a few inches above toaster and heat for 20 seconds or until powder melts, or use an embossing heat gun. Let cool 5 minutes.

5. **ASSEMBLE CARD.** Lay card flat, gilded side up, with flap at left. Center embossed image facedown within window opening. Trim away excess vellum, allowing ¼" margin all around. Using Yes Stikflat glue, affix vellum to window frame, then glue on window panel, gilded side up, sandwiching vellum in between. Fold flap in, and apply short piece of invisible tape to lower end (illustration C). Press one gold star on tape. Weight under heavy book overnight. Write your own greeting on red surface of card with gold metallic pen. To use card, open into box shape, and seal flap with star. Set over votive candle placed in a glass holder (illustration D).

C. Gild the inside, and add a vellum insert.

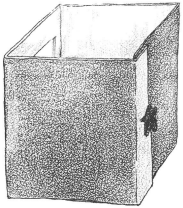

D. Close the flap with the self-stick star.

Making the Envelope

1. **CUT CARDSTOCK.** Lay enlarged envelope pattern on red cardstock. Using T-pin, pierce each inner and outer point of perimeter (12 pinholes total). Connect pinholes dot-to-dot to draft envelope outline. Cut on marked lines.

2. **ASSEMBLE ENVELOPE.** Fold in four flaps in order indicated on pattern. Open flat. Brush Yes Stikflat glue on outer edges of bottom triangle. Fold in side flaps, fold up bottom flap, and press to adhere. Weight under heavy book overnight. Insert folded card, and seal top flap closed with self-adhesive star. Write name or greeting on face of envelope with gold metallic pen.

ENVELOPE PATTERN

NOTE: Photocopy
pattern at 200%.

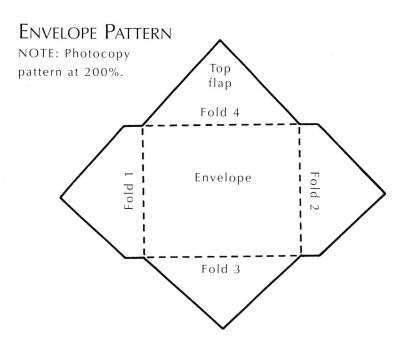

Sources

Charrette
31 Olympia Avenue
Woburn, MA 01888
(800)367-3729
www.charrette.com
Printing blocks and Speedball water-based inks

Home Cake Decorating Supply Company
9514 Roosevelt Way NE
Seattle, WA 98115
(206)522-4300
Luster Dust, edible glitter, gold dragées, plastic squeeze bottles with couplers

Pearl Paint
308 Canal Street
New York, NY 10013
(800)451-PEARL
www.pearlpaint.com
Rolco Labs reflective beads

Rings and Things
PO Box 450
Spokane, WA 99210-0450
(800)366-2156
www.Rings-Things.com
Flatback Austrian crystal rhinestones

Super Silk
PO Box 527596
Flushing, NY 11352
(800)432-SILK
Silk dupioni, metallic organza